Fashion for Free

Written and illustrated by Janet Allen
Photographs by Michael Cooper

PENGUIN BOOKS

Penguin Books Ltd, Harmondsworth,
Middlesex, England
Penguin Books, 625 Madison Avenue,
New York, New York 10022, U.S.A.
Penguin Books Australia Ltd, Ringwood,
Victoria, Australia
Penguin Books Canada Ltd, 2801 John Street,
Markham, Ontario, Canada L3R 1B4
Penguin Books (N.Z.) Ltd, 182–190 Wairau Road,
Auckland 10, New Zealand

First published in Peacock Books 1980

Phototypeset in Great Britain by
Filmtype Services Limited, Scarborough
Printed in Great Britain
by Hazell Watson & Viney Ltd, Aylesbury, Bucks.

PEACOCK BOOKS

Fashion for Free

Janet Allen attended the Kingston School of Art and the Royal College of Art, and later taught adult education, in art schools and in a school for maladjusted children. For seven years she ran a small firm which designed, screen-printed and produced household and fashion items. She is now a freelance writer and illustrator, describing herself as 'addicted to junk shopping and jumbling'. Janet Allen has also written *Exciting Things To Do With Colour* and *Step-by-step Pictures* for children, both of which have been translated into several languages.

Contents

Acknowledgements

I am especially grateful to Susan Bader for her assistance in preparing this book.

I would also like to thank the following people for their kind help and uncomplaining cooperation:

Rozz Connor
Wendy Roberts
Nicky Marsh
Michelle Marsh
Jacky Hinton
Clare Whitney
Lorna Green
Melody Morris
Beverley Dublin
Trevor George
Pamela Kraus
Jo Kaupe
Paul Grundy
David Knight
Gwen Smith
Stella Oake
Jane Callender
Karen Lee
Wendy Crease
Gillian Allan
Peter Hall

What's this book about?

This book is for people who want their clothes to put across their personalities – but who haven't the inclination, the know-how or the money that conventional dressmaking demands. The book shows you how to make and decorate garments – either those you've made or old drearies lurking in the wardrobe – in lots of unusual ways.

There are no complicated graphs or charts here. The easy-going garments are designed to fit all sizes and the sewing methods suggested are the easiest and most straightforward.

We are all gobbling up our poor world's natural resources at an alarming rate, minute by minute. Partly because of this, new fabrics and paper patterns have become incredibly expensive. So it seems a very good and economical idea to recycle materials into clothing. There are plenty of suggestions here on how to acquire materials really cheaply (legally).

Materials

Some ways of acquiring materials – cheaply

Your wardrobe may already consist of garments desperately waiting to be re-vitalized but you'll probably need some additional materials.

Some things – dyes, for example – you will have to buy in the usual way. Reliable suppliers are listed at the back of this book. If you write off for information, catalogues, etc., people do appreciate your enclosing a stamped, self-addressed envelope for the reply. With certain products like iron-on bonding material (no sewing), it might be sensible and economical to share the cost and the material with a friend.

Do make your interests known to all and sundry.

It's amazing how Uncle Bertie will suddenly remember he's got some old lino-cutters in the loft he hasn't used for twenty years and you're welcome to them. Mrs King-down-the-baker's has a length of gingham she bought in a sale – and still hasn't done anything with it. 'More use to you, dear, than it is to me' . . . etc. . . . etc.

Then there's always your birthday and Christmas. Free materials are the best of all. But if you've got to pay, explore the following avenues.

The two dresses on the left are both based on a standard bought paper pattern. The one on the left is made up out of different scraps of crêpe fabric, many of them sample pieces. The other is made in a cheap cotton remnant. The decoration on the bust was cut out of a chair cover.

The dress on the right is made out of an old curtain. The collar was a remnant and all the lace trimmings came from an old tablecloth.

Jumble and rummage sales

Jumbles, being amateur fund-raising events, are invariably staffed by kindly sales people, only too willing to help. It's really the other customers you should be wary of – experienced old hands who've spent years perfecting the technique. To avoid being crushed to a pulp in the general stampede, observe the following few rules.

The law of the jumble

1 *He/she who hesitates is lost.*
2 *Be firm, but polite. Physically this takes the form of giving as good as you get with the elbows, whilst smiling at your opponent. Verbally it means that haggling pleasantly over the price is quite acceptable (the time-honoured tradition of the souks).*
3 *Always have your money handy, in coins of small denomination. Valuable hunting time may be lost whilst the vicar is sought, he being the only person present with change for a fiver.*
4 *Take a sensible bag, preferably with a shoulder strap, thereby leaving both hands free for rummaging.*
5 *Keep an open mind. Remember that the seasons inevitably change. Although it may be sweltering today, there will come a time when that fur collar could be truly welcome.*
6 *Keep your eyes open. There are frequently little treasures under the table or in the penny-box. Look out for interesting buttons, buckles, etc. The garment they adorn may be hideous – well, rags are always useful.*
7 *On returning home, make sure you sort out, clean and store the bits you want to keep. Smelly heaps of old clothing left around the house are not likely to further your cause.*

Charity shops

The prices in charity shops, like Oxfam, will be a bit higher than at jumble sales but they are well worth browsing through.

Secondhand shops and stalls

Be careful here. The proprietor may well be wised up to the latest trends in nostalgia and some of the old clothes could cost a fortune. These are, after all, commercial concerns. As the customer, it's up to you to examine the goods properly and make your own decision. Just be wary of slick patter. Think twice and reject it if a jumper, despite its lovely pattern, is horribly matted under the arms and riddled with moth holes. The salesman's description of 'nicely worn in' may well be another way of saying 'nastily worn out'. Check seams, under-arms, collars. If they are torn or rotting it may be wiser to give up that particular garment. Is there a good hem? Extra fabric here can be useful.

Remnant sales

Very often the remnants in the soft furnishing department of a big store are much cheaper than the reduced dress fabrics. You can find some very useful plain linings to paint or print on. Also ends of lines in household linens are sometimes exceedingly cheap – blankets, sheets, etc.

Army surplus shops

This type of shop is often worth looking around. You'll find some well-made garments, especially sporty, outdoor stuff. Some may be a good basis for your own individual decoration.

Swatches (sample fabrics)

Ask in soft furnishing shops or departments and tailors' shops for their out-of-date swatches – great for patchworking.

Workshop throw-aways

If you live near a mill where fabrics are made, or a tailor's workshop, make inquiries to see if they have any scrap material to give away.

Toy shops

Excellent for delicious beads and silly decoration ideas.

Craft shops

These are more expensive, of course – but just the sort of place where you could choose your next birthday present.

Felt

Craft, needlework and haberdashery shops sell small squares of felt in beautiful colours so you don't have to buy a big piece of material when you only need a tiny bit – a patch, for instance. Cadging from a craft teacher is another approach to be considered.

Leather and suede

If you see leather or suede garments in a jumble sale buy them. Look out for old handbags too. You can even discover delights like real snakeskin. In the shops all skins are astronomically priced. If your jumble bargains are beyond wearing or re-vamping the material can be used for making patches, bindings, belts, bags.

If you live anywhere near a tannery you can probably buy unwanted scraps of suede or leather very cheaply. A factory where leather things are made up might let you have some off-cuts for nothing (ask nicely with your most winning smile).

Bespoke shoemakers and cobblers may change a little, but can sometimes produce lovely small bits too.

Wool

Like everything else, new wool and synthetic yarns are now very expensive. You may find the odd ball or two considerably reduced when it comes to sale time. Look out for these because there's usually not enough of any one colour to make anything much more than a single mitten, but they're ideal if you only need a small amount for embroidery, or for knitting squares.

Unwanted woollen garments, providing they are not worn out, can be unpicked. Washing really re-vitalizes the wool and it can then be used again. Don't use sweaters, etc., that have machine-sewn seams. They are

too difficult to undo. You will cut the wool by mistake and end up with lots of short lengths rather than lovely hanks. So go for hand-made garments at jumbles and charity shops. Or, even cheaper, ask your friends and relations for their cast-offs.

This is what you do. With care undo all the seams. Track down the casting-off end of each piece of the garment and start to unravel the wool. It will look very Afro-crinkly at this stage but it dries straight after being washed. As you undo it wind the wool round the back of a chair to form a hank.

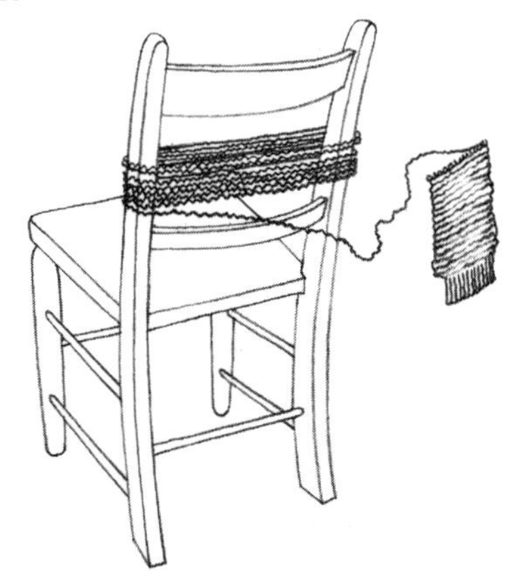

When the hank reaches a size that will be easy to wash, tie it round (not tightly) with short lengths of wool. This is to prevent it becoming an uncontrollable nightmare when you wash it. Tie it in four places like this with wool of a different colour – easy to find when you want to undo it later. Lift the hank off the chair back.

When all the wool has been wound into hanks and tied, wash it by hand with care. Use a fabric conditioner, rinse and then hang it out on the washing line.

After it's thoroughly dried, wind the wool fairly loosely into balls. Once again use the chair back or, even better, a willing slave.

Wool can also be dyed, should you wish to change its colour. Check with the general dyeing information on page 142 for the types of dye, etc. Dye the wool, still in its hanks, after you have washed and thoroughly rinsed it.

Cleaning and storing your finds

Sort out which bits and pieces are going to be useful to you. Don't store secondhand things without cleaning them first. If you only need bits of a garment, cut off those bits to clean them and discard the rest.

Wash according to the fabric type. With silks, other delicate fabrics and woollies use a mild soap (like Lux) or a washing liquid (like Stergene) and wash by hand. Fabric conditioner is recommended, especially for woollens. Cottons and other tough fabrics, providing the colours are fast, can be machine or hand washed in detergent.

WARNING! *Biological detergents can devour buttons* (*bone ones*).

Don't put leather or suede in a coin-op dry cleaning machine. It turns into hardboard. It's very expensive to have leather dry-cleaned professionally, so indulge in this only if you've bought a real gem. You can successfully wash real leather (and some suede) by hand in mild soap or washing liquid. Do it on a sunny, windy day so that it can dry quickly out of doors. When the leather is dry rub in shoe polish of an appropriate colour all over and buff it up with a soft brush and a rag. Chamois leather can be washed too. (This has a suede-like finish, so don't polish it.) There are some washable suedes. If you can test a piece of something for washability do so. When it's dry brush the nap up with a suede brush. If in doubt, consult a dry cleaner.

An ancient method of cleaning dark-coloured fur is to use bran (not All Bran). Buy some at a pet shop or horse and cattle feed merchant's. It's a good idea to perform this operation outside – the birds will appreciate it too. First warm the bran up in the oven (not piping hot) and then sprinkle it thickly all over the fur. Rub it well in. Then shake and gently beat the fur to get rid of every trace of bran. It takes the dirt with it. Finally brush the fur.

For white or pale-coloured fur sprinkle on flour (ordinary baking flour). Leave it on for an hour and then shake and beat the fur to remove the powder (and the dirt). Give it a final brushing.

Store your cut-off zips, buckles, ribbons, belts, etc., in a box or a drawer, keeping them all together so that you can find things when you need them. Buttons look decorative kept in a big glass jar (and you can see what you've got).

If you are short of space, why not stuff cushions with the pieces of fabric and garments that are awaiting attention?

General Info

Sewing gear

Any special tools or equipment are mentioned as you go along but the absolute basic sewing requirements are:

Something to sew with – a machine if one is available; anyway, a packet of assorted hand-sewing needles so that you'll have suitable ones for different jobs.

Dressmaker's pins. Endeavour to keep them in something that doesn't fall over all the time – what about a pin cushion? Spend a little bit extra and buy stainless steel lace or silk pins. Being stainless steel they are strong and won't rust and will therefore last for ever; being silk pins they are slender and won't leave great holes in fine fabrics.

A decent sharp pair of scissors. These are to be used ONLY on fabric and when not in use, should be concealed in a very secret place, known only to yourself.

A small pair of pointed scissors, such as nail scissors, are handy too.

A flexible tape measure. Those with metal ends are best, otherwise the first and last centimetres rapidly fade away.

Tailor's chalk for drawing on cloth. This is most convenient in pencil form. Some even have a little brush on the end. The lines you draw brush off the fabric when you no longer require them.

An iron, an ironing board or table and some scrap cotton fabric to use as a damp cloth.

Simple methods

All the garments in this book can be made by machine or by hand.

Explaining the different stitches

To begin a row of hand sewing thread the needle, tie a knot at the end of the thread and proceed. These are the stitches you will come across.

Tacking

This means long in-and-out temporary stitches, just to hold something in place until the final sewing.

Running stitch

Little in-and-out stitches as even and small as possible, like mini tacking, but this time permanent. Both tacking and running should be finished off with a couple of stitches of backstitch.

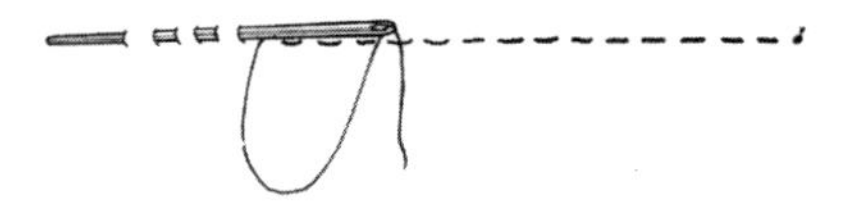

Backstitch

As the name implies, this means doing a stitch and then going back on it like this:

Again, make the stitches as even and small as possible. It's a very strong stitch.

The word 'backstitching' is also used about machine sewing. In order to secure the beginning and the end of a line of machining always do a few backstitches. In machine terms, this means going in reverse. Modern machines have a button or a lever to put the machine into reverse but ancient machines won't go backwards. The trick here is to lift the foot whilst the needle is still through the material. Don't tug on the fabric or you may break the needle. Just swing the material round and lower the foot so that you can then machine in the opposite direction to the one in which you were going.

Hemming

Like tiny oversewing (see page 21) to fasten a turning down.

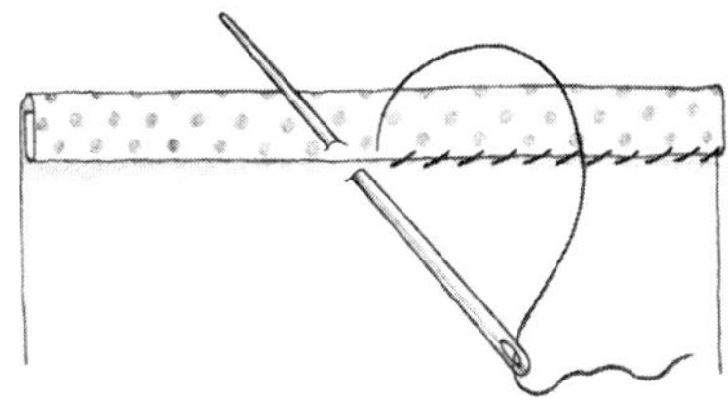

Adhesives

Although fabric adhesive may look like the answer to all your problems, be warned by this true story. A friend, thinking along these very same lines, made an entire ensemble – jacket and skirt in tweed – all stuck together with glue. This she frequently wore and it was much admired. The day came for it to be dry-cleaned and so she duly deposited it at the cleaners. After the appropriate time had elapsed, my friend surrendered her ticket.

'Your suit, madam,' sneered the assistant, handing her a neat pile of immaculate pieces of fabric.

So – just confine your gluing to the less vital areas like decorative patches; or use adhesive as a back-up to stitching.

Rubber-based gum is recommended for things like hems on leather garments, where there is no strain on it.

Iron-ons

You sandwich an iron-on bonding material between two fabrics that are to be joined – no sewing. The heat and the pressure on the iron melts the contents of the sandwich and fuses the fabrics together. There are various iron-ons for various purposes, so make sure you've got the right one. The webbing type, in a strip, has no backing. (An example is Newey's Fusible Hemming Web.) This is especially for sticking hems up – but you can cut bits off to use for smaller jobs. For a hem, make a single turning. This means you never have a bulky hem and at the same time the bonding material seals the raw edge. A similar material comes in a sheet with a temporary paper backing. This is handy, particularly for appliqué and patching, because you can draw or trace shapes on to the paper and then cut them out. By positioning the shapes sensibly you can make your bonding material last for ages.

Iron-on interfacing is only sticky on one side. It is for adding 'body' to a fabric, i.e. it makes it stronger.

All the iron-ons are available in chain stores and haberdashers. Follow the instructions on the packet carefully or you may end up with the iron firmly glued to your trousers. (If this *does* happen, use a non-metal pot-scourer to clean the iron.)

How to neaten the edges of the seams

Finishing off the edges of the seams after you've made a garment is rather a pain. You need not do so if the material is very firmly woven and shows no sign of fraying. If, however, it is of the fraying variety you must steel yourself to apply one of the following treatments; that is if you want your garment to remain in one piece.

The only kind of seam you need to make up all the things in this book is the plain seam. That's just a line of sewing joining two pieces of fabric together, generally 1·5cm in from the edge. The finished seam is pressed open flat on the wrong side of the garment. If the fabric is not going to fray you can leave it at that. Otherwise . . .

Pinking

Pinking shears are those scissors with zigzag blades. Borrow a pair if you need to and simply trim the very edge of the seams. Pinking is best for a closely woven material that's not going to be washed frequently.

Machine zigzagging

If your machine will zigzag this is a very easy way of finishing off a seam and it will do for any kind of material.

Oversewing

Hand sew sloping stitches over the raw edges of a seam.

Blanket stitch

This is very versatile because it can be used for neatening the edges of a seam or a hem (and, if worked close together, a buttonhole) and it can also act as a bold, decorative embroidery stitch. Use a thick thread – wool, for example. The stitches can be quite long, 2cm, say, in thick wool. Start off by bringing the thread through to the right side of the fabric at the top of a stitch and down to the edge. Make a little stitch at the edge. Then back to the top again but this time pass the needle through the loop of thread – and you're off.

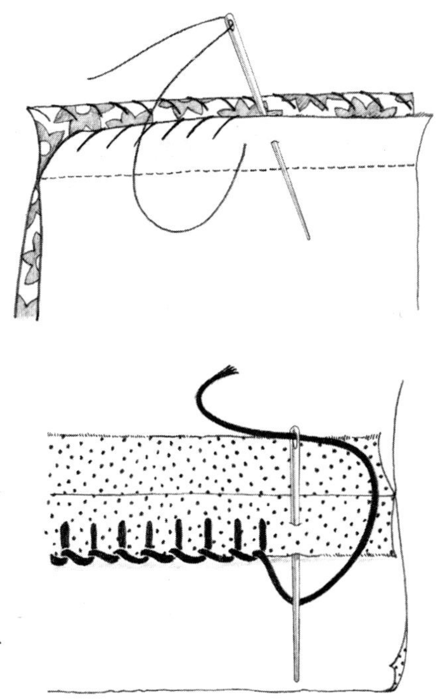

Cheap and easy fastenings

Save money and be creative by making your own cords, etc., to use as fastening and trimming materials.

Pin-ups

That wondrous invention the safety-pin is the easiest of all methods of fastening one piece of cloth to another but it is, unfortunately, somewhat frowned upon in polite society. So (if you move in polite society) get round this by employing exactly the same principle and using a super brooch, a zany pin-on button or a magnificent military badge (as on this cape, also illustrated on page 67).

That's fine if you need to fasten a garment at one point only. Frequently though, a whole front needs joining together. Investigate some of the following solutions.

Buttoned up

If you've no objection to sewing on buttons and making buttonholes – OK. Page 36 shows you the principle of hand sewing a buttonhole. If you have a modern machine that does buttonholes consult the handbook. Obviously, whatever the method, you must make the hole fit snugly round the button. For the idle among us, here's a quick (and lasting) way of making a buttonhole, using iron-on fusible web. Cut a slit the length of the buttonhole plus two tiny V cuts at the ends:

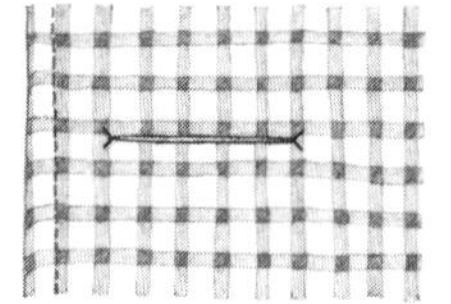

Turn the long sides of the slit under to the wrong side of the fabric and stick them well and truly down by the approved method (see both page 19 and the packet instructions). So you'll have this on the wrong side:

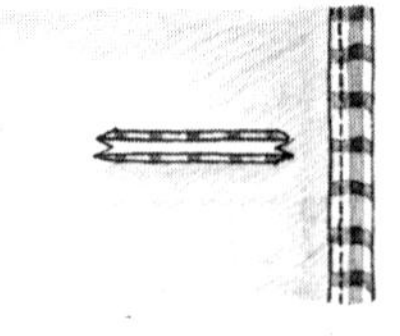

Iron and stick down those little end V bits too. From the right side the completed buttonhole looks like this:

Loops instead of holes are another way of fastening buttons. You can sew cord along the edge of a garment opposite the buttons. An alternative method is first to sew a number of threads, making the loop, and then to go over it with buttonhole or blanket stitch.

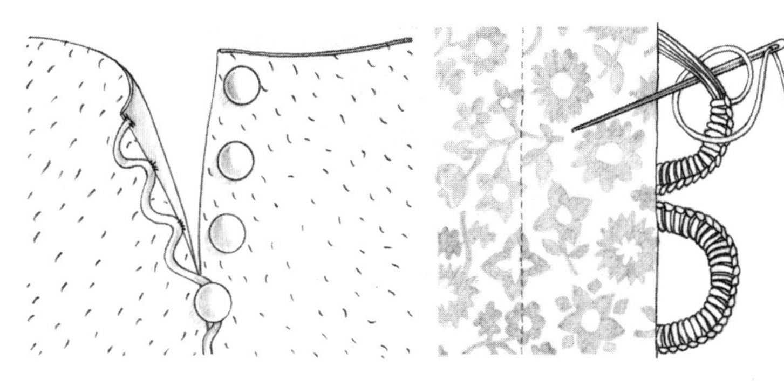

Cord figure-of-eight loops can be applied to pairs of buttons. Join the cord and stitch it to the fabric so that it is concealed behind one of the buttons.

General Info

There are some easy-to-do cheap button covering kits on the market, available in Woolworths and other shops. Just follow the instructions carefully. Do-it-yourself leather-covered buttons are spectacular. (At last a use for that solitary suede glove.) Use only the largest size button for leather, though; the smaller ones won't grip it properly. A useful tip is to dampen the cloth or leather before applying it to the button shell.

A further sloth's delight is the jeans button, now available to the public via Woolworths. These are in different metallic finishes or black. This button consists of two parts, a top button-shaped piece and a bit at the back with a ribbed spike sticking up. You just put the spike through the material from the wrong side and firmly press the other section on to it by hand.

For the truly dedicated lazy-bones Newey's Buttonsnaps are the answer. These also are sold in Woolworths. The basic idea is a covered button on a snap fastener – no buttonholes to worry about. They are clearly best suited to a garment that's always worn buttoned up. Otherwise, where other people have buttonholes you'll have shiny discs – revealing your secret.

Tied up

Clothing can look most attractive fastened with ties made of braid, cord, leather, bootlace, etc. Suitable lengths are sewn on in corresponding pairs. You tie them as you wish – tightly, loosely, in bows or in knots. Attaching ties in conjunction with binding a garment is explained in the waistcoat section on page 74.

Lacing up

Lacing the pieces of a garment together has great possibilities. Make eyelet holes (page 54) or loops, and experiment with different ways of lacing up. Criss-crossing various coloured cords could be fun.

Hooked up

Giant-size fabric-covered hooks and eyes that are intended for fur coats look very decorative. Sew them on what is, in fact, the wrong way round – and maybe add some fancy embroidery too.

You could work a similar ruse with the clips off the ends of an old pair of braces (or some newly bought clips – they are quite cheap). Sew the clip to one side of the garment and, as that end of the clip is a bit thin and weedy, embellish it in some way with ribbon threaded through or some embroidery. Then simply open the clip, slide the other side of the garment in, and snap the clip shut.

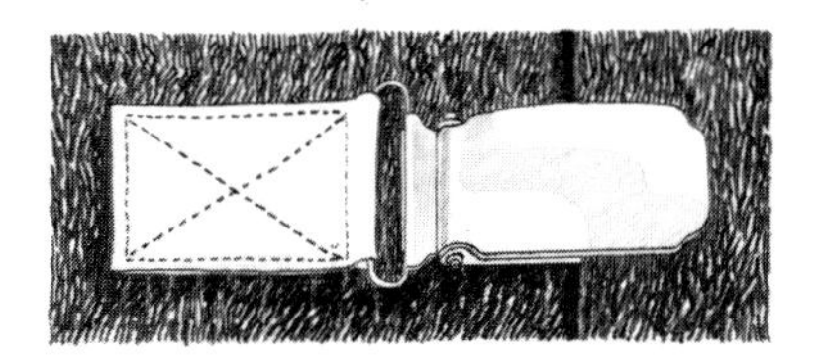

Belt up

This is rather smart. Cut off the business ends of a belt (or a selection of belts) and sew them on as fastening devices.

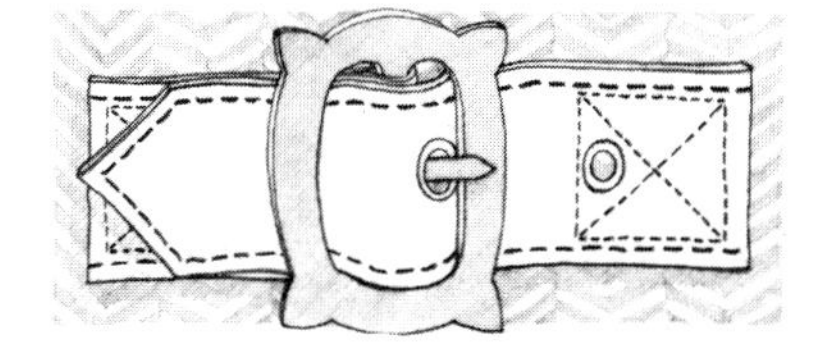

Press-ups

There are now lots of different kinds of hammer-in press studs with nice brass or patterned finishes. There's also tape in various widths with press studs spaced along it. Have a good look round your local shops to see what answers your particular problem. When applying these do read the instructions carefully. It's important to get all the bits lined up properly before hammering.

Woollen cord

This is how to make woollen cord. Medium-weight wool makes a cord that's fine for lacing things up or for use as a decorative piping. Rug wool makes a super thick cord suitable for a belt.

Here is the technique. Decide on the length you want your cord to be and add on approximately 10cm (that will get lost in the knots). Cut two pieces of wool twice this length and knot them together at either end.

Loop one end round something fairly thin that's not going to move – a cup hook, for example. Thread the other end through a cotton reel and then push a pencil through the very end, up by the knot. Hold the wool out taut with one hand behind the cotton reel. With the other hand turn the pencil round and round, propeller-style.

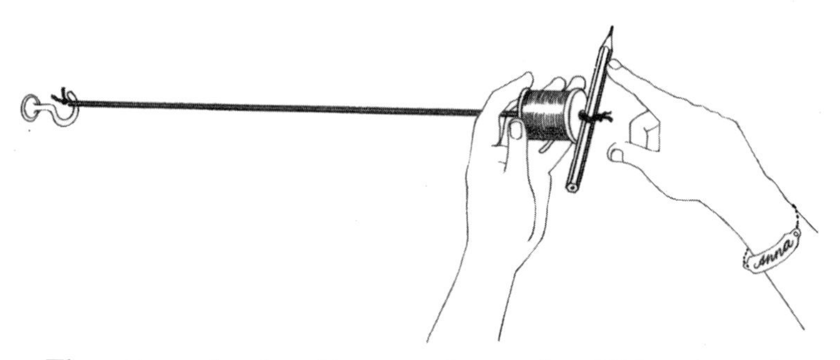

The cotton reel makes this a smooth operation. Without it you keep banging the pencil and your finger into your other hand.

Twist the wool up really tightly until it practically starts to twist up on itself again. Slide the end off the hook, being careful to keep a tight hold on it.

Remove the pencil and the cotton reel – without allowing the wool to unwind. Let go of the wool and it will double back on itself, leaping into a thicker cord. Knot the loose ends together. By smoothing with the fingers neaten out any odd-looking bumps, should any occur.

A thicker cord can be made with four, instead of two, lengths of wool. On a cord made from a loosely spun wool you can make a lovely silky tassel by teasing out the fringe below the knot with a wire brush, such as you use for suede shoes. Woolly pompons make a different finish too. If you like the idea of the odd bead here and there along the cord thread them on in the first stage, before you start twisting. Distribute them along half the length of the wool because when it doubles back it naturally becomes half its original length. The beads end up neatly held within the cord.

Plaiting

You can plait long strips of anything together – wool, string, leather, ribbon or fabric. Combine them or keep to just one type of material. Work in beads too, if the mood takes you.

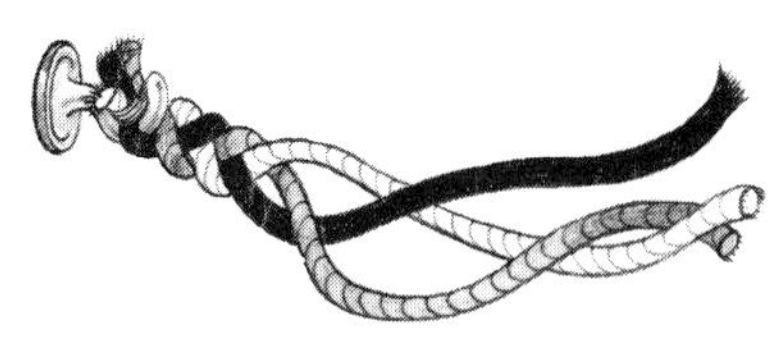

Either bind tightly round or knot the three strands of the plait at one end and attach it to a hook. Plait in the traditional way as with hair, keeping it nice and even. Finish off with a knot or more binding.

There are lots of different possibilities in plaiting fabric strips. Join the fabric if necessary to make it long enough. The width of the strip depends upon the type of fabric being used and what it's for. You'll have to experiment but a rough guide is that a plait of 3cm wide strips of cotton sheeting will give you a cord of approximately dressing gown cord thickness.

So that you avoid horrible frayed bits sticking out iron the strips first like this to enclose the raw edges:

Materials that do fray a lot are to be avoided. Jersey fabrics are particularly suited to plaiting, but keep the tension the same if using it with a non-stretch fabric, or the jersey will stretch and cause cockling.

Chinese ball buttons

This is really a piece of cord tied in an elaborate knot. A 28cm length of dressing gown cord ends up as a ball button measuring approximately 1·5cm across – that's allowing a bit to spare, which you trim off afterwards.

Here's what you do. It's easiest to do this flat on the table, rather than in the air. First make a loop.

Then make a second loop that goes over the first and then under the lead-in part of the first loop.

Now bring the cord up as if to make a third loop but this time thread it in and out of the other two loops.

Pull the ends up gently and mould the knot into a nice ball. Trim off the ends, leaving sufficient to sew the button to the garment at the back of the ball.

Tassels

These are fun on the ends of cord belts or sewn directly on to things – little ones all over a sweater, for example.

Get a piece of card which is the length of the tassel and just wind wool (or yarn) round and round the card, until you think it's thick enough. Tie a thread tightly through the top end. Cut through all the wool at the bottom end. Then, to make the little bobble at the top, wrap some wool round and round the whole tassel, just a little way down from the top. Tie it and lose the ends in the general fringing.

There could be some attractive variations here – tying round in different colours, introducing metallic thread, and so on.

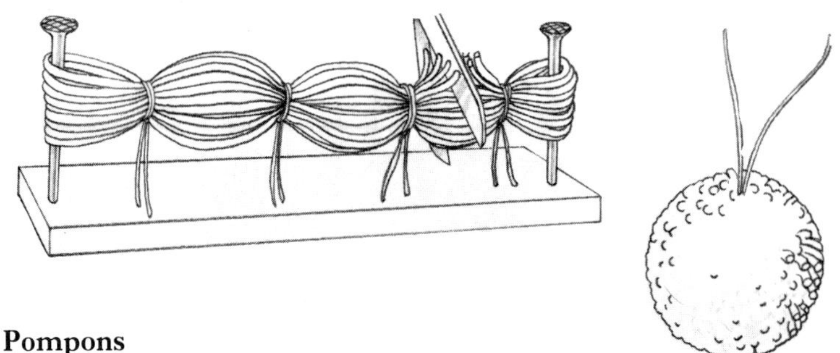

Pompons

This is a very quick method of making little bobbles, which can be used in much the same way as tassels. Hammer two nails into a strip of wood (or use two conveniently spaced hooks) and wind a thick hank of yarn around them. Tie thread exceedingly tightly round the hank at intervals, leaving the two ends of thread trailing. Cut through the hank halfway between the tied points to make a pompon. Roll it into a good round shape, trimming it if necessary. Use the two long ends of thread to fasten it on.

Temporary first-aid for zips

One of the cruel facts of life is that zips break. Any book on dressmaking will show you how to insert a new zip. However if the teeth snap or get out of alignment at the bottom end of the zip you can do a bodge-up job which, if handled with care, will last for months. This is only any good if you can wriggle yourself in and out of the garment with the zip opened just as far down as the broken part and no further (so lay off the Danish pastries).

On the inside of the zip, just a tooth or two above the broken section, push a safety-pin through the fabric edging on one side of the zip, across the teeth at the front and back again through the fabric edging on the other side. Fasten the safety-pin. This forms a little bar and the zip cannot open beyond it. From the outside it's virtually invisible.

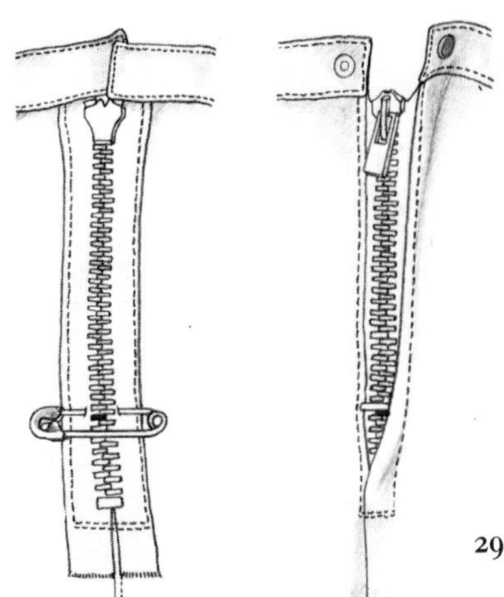

Your personal measurements

Ask a friend to help you fill in the chart on page 32. It will be useful both for making up garments and for knowing your size when you buy things. With ready-to-wear clothes it's hopeless going by the label sizes, which differ from one brand to another.

Fill in the chart in pencil so that, should you extend in any direction or have a violent fit of slimming, you can just rub out the original figures and replace them.

Stand up straight in bare feet, wearing your usual bra and pants – and don't cheat.

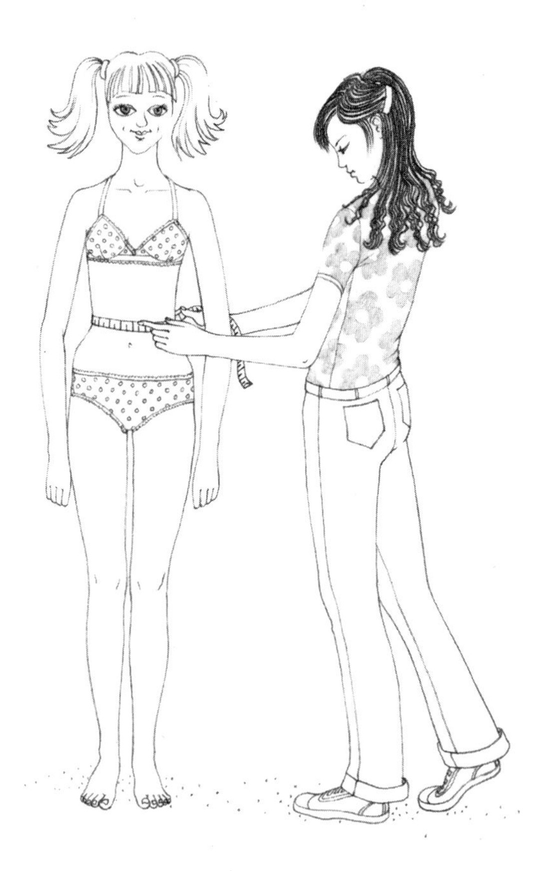

Bust (or, on a guy, chest). Wrap the tape-measure round the fullest part of the bust (or chest), snugly but not tight. Make sure the tape is not drooping down at the back.

Waist. Keeping the tape-measure horizontal, wrap it around the narrowest part of the waist.

Hips. The tape-measure must go (regrettably perhaps) around the fattest part of the hips. Keep it horizontal, not up and over the bottom.

Back waist length. Bend your head forward and you'll feel a knobble sticking out at the nape of your neck. Take this measurement straight down the centre of your back from the knobble to your waist.

Front waist length. This is measured from the dip you have at the base of your neck down to the waist.

Shoulder. Lay the end of the tape on the point where your neck joins on to your shoulder and measure out to the bone you can feel on the outside of the shoulder.

Sleeve length. Bend your arm and measure from the shoulder bone, round the bent elbow, to your wrist bone. That's for a full-length sleeve. For shorter sleeves, obviously you must decide on the position of the cuff.

Inside leg. Measure from the crutch straight down the leg to the fashionable length for trousers.

These are all finished size measurements. Don't forget when sewing that you must add on the seam allowance.

Now measure your long-suffering friend.

Measurement chart

BUST (OR CHEST) ....

WAIST ....

HIPS ....

BACK WAIST LENGTH ....

FRONT WAIST LENGTH ....

SHOULDER ....

SLEEVE LENGTH ....

INSIDE LEG ....

Garments to make

The easiest pattern in the world – a poncho

This is the basic poncho shape, as worn by any self-respecting Mexican bandit. Here it is made from an old blanket – really snug. And yet here too is exactly the same pattern (merely longer) made up out of a floaty piece of silk picked up at a jumble sale and tie-dyed – an amazingly sophis-

ticated evening dress. The same shape becomes a super beach cover-up if recycled towels are used. And when it's not covering you up – you stretch out on it for sun bathing. Make it any length you like, to be a dress or a top; in any fabric you like. In something like denim it makes a great unisex messing-about-in-boats sort of smock. Made from PVC or shower-proof nylon it's ideal in the rain.

The shape is a rectangle with a slit in the middle for your head to go through. Calculate the size of the rectangle like this. Measure the length you want the poncho to be from the nape of the neck down. The complete poncho rectangle will be twice this length – the front plus the back. The width is measured from the base of the neck, where the shoulder starts, along the outside of the crooked arm to the distance you require. The Mexican-type poncho width goes as far as the wrist, the dress only just past the elbow. Either you, or the fabric you have available, will decide this length. The full width of the rectangle is twice this measurement.

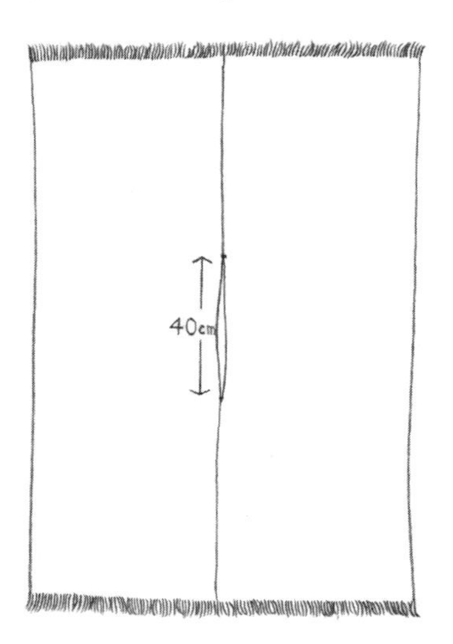

It's easiest of all to make a poncho out of two long strips of fabric with the two edges that join in the centre being selvedges. Obviously, this automatically makes a lovely neat seam. Find the centre of the poncho and mark 20cm either side of it, making a total of 40cm, which you leave unsewn for the neck hole. Sew the two pieces together. Don't forget the backstitching to secure each end of the neck hole. The edges of the neck hole just need single turning and hemming. Turn and hem the outside edges of the poncho or finish them in a fancy way by binding or adding fringes or embroidery. If the edges at the centre join are not selvedges, you'll have to double turn and hem the edges of the neck hole.

Similarly four towels can be joined, first into two long strips, and then into a poncho as above.

If you are making your poncho from one complete rectangle of material, treat the neck slit as a giant buttonhole. Consider first a poncho in a heavy blanket type of fabric, as this material is thick enough to need no reinforcing. Find the centre point of the poncho and rule a 20cm line either side of it – 40cm in all. Fold the poncho in half. Pinching the fabric together, cut 2cm or so down along the drawn line through the double fabric. Open the poncho out. You can easily slide the scissors into the slit and neatly cut the rest of it.

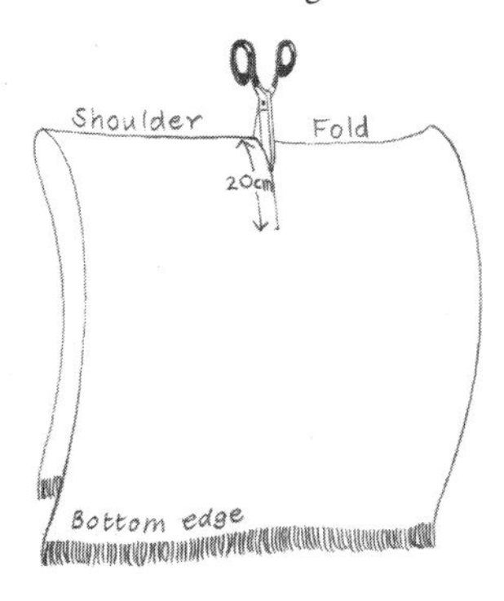

Using thick wool, perhaps in a super contrasting colour, hand sew the raw edge of the slit. Do blanket stitch (page 21) worked close together all along each side. At the ends sew two or three long straight stitches across. Then neatly cover these with small oversewing.

Doing this may well give you a taste for embroidery and you might end up decorating the whole of your poncho. Have a look at the embroidery section of this book for some stimulating ideas.

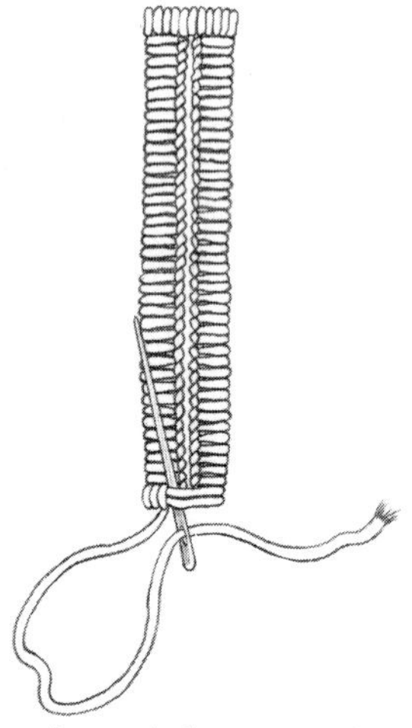

On a lightweight fabric a bit of extra thickness is needed to strengthen the neck area. Cut a long narrow strip of thin material 44 × 4cm. Draw the central 40cm line on the right side of the poncho. Put a line of pins or tacking through it so that it is also clear on the wrong side. Attach the long strip to the wrong side of the poncho either with fabric adhesive or iron-on bonding material. Make sure the 40cm line is precisely centred. Cut the slit through the two layers of cloth and work buttonhole stitch as described above. Use a thread that suits the type of garment. Bright, thick peasanty cotton thread for a sporty, outdoor top; a more elegant silk thread for an evening dress.

Page 22 describes an alternative way of making a slit with no stitching, entirely iron-on.

Add a pocket

How about adding a big front double pocket? Cut out a rectangle 35 × 20cm. Turn and hem it all the way round. Pin it to the front of the poncho, being sure to centre it, and sew it on along the top and bottom edges and vertically right through the middle.

Poncho dress

If you want to use the poncho pattern for a dress or smock top, rather than as an outer garment, you'll want to avoid arrest for indecent exposure by sewing up the sides. This is quite straightforward. Fold the poncho in half. Pin the side seams from the bottom to within 35cm or so of the top fold. Try it on and adjust the sleeve holes to your liking. Sew up the side seams, turn and hem the sleeve edges.

Here is an attractive variation, with a tie belt.

Put the garment on and with tailor's chalk mark the two points under the bust between which gathering looks best. In exactly the same way as for the neck slit, make two little buttonholes at these points. Thread a sash or cord through. You can then wear the dress with a gathered front and loose back. Make two equivalent holes at the back and you can have a gathered back too, or a gathered back and a loose front.

Poncho tunic

The fabric you have acquired may mean that a poncho with a horizontal neckline going from shoulder to shoulder, rather than from nape to chest, is more sensible. Consider this before you start hacking away at your material. This elegant poncho tunic is made with a horizontal neckline from two jumble-bought lace curtains.

A tunic like this in a lacy fabric – even quite mundane old lace curtains – can be trimmed by threading coloured ribbons in and out. It's an almost instant solution to the 'Good grief, I've nothing to wear' response that usually accompanies an unexpected invitation. You simply wear it, belted or flowing, over something you've had for years and the effect looks like a totally new outfit.

Shirring – some ideas for summer

Do you fancy some light, easy-going warm-weather clothes – nice for casual wear during the day but sophisticated enough for evening barbecues and summer parties?

Things in the shops are so expensive and the rate at which you seem to be growing makes buying new clothing a very uneconomical proposition.

Have a good hunt round for something made of a *lightweight* fabric that you can recycle as a dress or a skirt and top. The skirt and top can be worn together or separately, so you can make just one of them if you haven't much material.

Try out shirring – sometimes called 'ruching'. It is a way of gathering up material by sewing on parallel lines of elastic. This means the shirred parts of the garment hug your body but they will also expand should you too expand. So shirred clothes are great for people who are growing fast.

Remember, the fabric must be lightweight in order to gather up properly. Enormous great thick gathers wouldn't be very flattering anyway.

Although patchwork is suggested in this book as a way of creating your own fabrics to make up into garments it is not a good idea to use shirring on it. Shirring done by machine only works properly on a single thickness of fabric. However, you could use patchworked areas on the parts of the garment that have no shirring on them, like the lower part of a skirt or dress.

How much material is required?

The amount of fabric you have determines what you can make so check this properly first.

For a skimpy top to fit a small or average size bust up to 86cm you will need two pieces of fabric the same size:

Don't worry about the pieces looking so wide. The shirring closes the fabric right up. You'll also need something to make the halter strap from which is a maximum of 56cm long – some suggestions: a football boot lace (these come in several different colours, so choose one to go with your fabric; a length of ribbon; a fabric plait (see page 26); a length of cord; wide rick-rack; or a strap made from the same fabric as the rest of the top. This sized top can be made from a pillow-case in nylon, cotton or polyester and you could make a skirt from a matching sheet. Coloured or patterned bed linen is very suitable, but if the only sheets and pillow-cases you can get were once white but have now gone a nasty grey try some plain or patterned dyeing (see pages 142–57).

Only make a skimpy top if your waist is fit to be seen. If the effect is likely to be something like the sketch on the right avoid it and go for a slightly longer version. It's kinder to the general public and anyway, who wants to turn people off needlessly?

For the longer type of top (as in the photographs), fitting up to a 91cm bust, you will require two pieces of fabric both the same size:

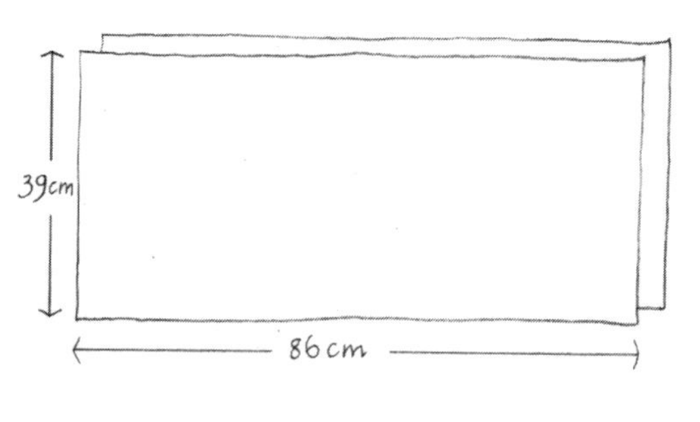

Two silky scarves would be ideal; and strap material as suggested previously. For a halter neck you will need a 56cm length. For straight straps two 51cm lengths are required.

To make a skirt you need two identical pieces of cloth that are 91cm wide × whatever length you want the skirt to be plus 9cm for turnings.

If you're having a frill along the bottom add on only 3·5 for turnings. The frill piece measures 367cm × the depth you choose. (Its length is twice that of the hem plus 3cm.) Each pocket is 25 × 20cm.

A dress takes two rectangular pieces of material:

A sheet or a large tablecloth will make an ankle-length dress. If you are just short of the full length but you can get an extra strip out of your piece of material complete the dress by adding a gathered frill along the bottom. This should measure whatever depth is required and be 367cm long. You can make it up by joining pieces if you need to. Strap materials, if straps are required, are the same as for the top.

How to do shirring, by machine and by hand

To shirr by machine you will need shirring elastic thread from a haberdashery shop, in addition to your normal machine thread. If you are using a recently made machine there will be details on how to do shirring in the instruction booklet, so follow these. If you have no such instructions you'll have to try a practice run on a spare bit of your fabric. This is to ensure that you have the tension and the length of the stitch correct. Wind the shirring elastic on to the bobbin by hand, stretching it as you wind. Slightly slacken both the bobbin and the upper tensions. Set the stitch length to 'large'. Try a line of stitching, sewing with the fabric right side up so that the elastic is underneath. If the upper thread pulls the elastic through the fabric, slacken the upper tension a bit more. Finish your line and pull the threads through to the wrong side and knot them. Being stretched under tension, the sewing might come undone if you didn't knot it like this. When you are working on a garment you will sew parallel lines of shirring 2cm apart.

To create the same effect with hand sewing you will need narrow 3mm wide flat elastic (knicker type). Sew the end of the elastic to the wrong side of the fabric. With ordinary sewing thread do herringbone stitches along either side of it:

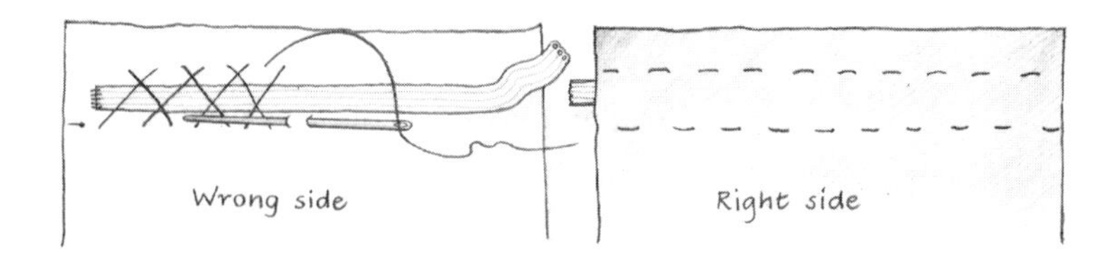

When you've reached the end pull the elastic up until the cloth is gathered up to the size you want, sew the loose end of elastic firmly to the fabric and cut it off just beyond the stitches.

How to make a top

Both styles of top are made in the same way. Having cut out the rectangles of fabric turn the top edge (that comes over the bust) under first 1cm and then 1·5cm. Pin this hem and sew it. Do exactly the same with the bottom edge.

Put the right sides of the material together and sew one of the side seams 1·5cm in. You now have a very wide rectangle. It is easier to do the shirring across a flat piece of fabric like this rather than round a tube – which is what you would have if you sewed both side seams at this stage. You will need some tailor's chalk (preferably in pencil form as it doesn't get blunt so quickly), a ruler and a long straight piece of wood, or something similar, to draw against. At either end of the long rectangle measure out and mark dots every 2cm down the short sides. Join up the dots by drawing straight chalk lines along your length of wood. If you are shirring by machine these lines should be on the right side of the fabric. (They brush off afterwards.) For shirring by hand chalk them on the wrong side.

Sew your shirring rows using the guide-lines. Be sure to finish each row off securely – you don't want it all pinging undone. When all the shirring is finished sew up the other side seam 1·5cm in. That's it – if it's a strapless top.

Straps

To add straps, first sew on one end of the strap (or straps) inside the top. Stitch it along the first row of the shirring. Put the top on and pull the strap (or straps) over to find out where the other end should go and how long the strap should be. Pin that other end. Remove the top, trim off the part of the strap that you don't need and sew the pinned end on firmly.

How to make a dress

The dress is made in just the same way as the top, so read and follow those instructions.

Pin and sew the top (over the bust) hem as explained previously. Sew up one of the side seams. If you're having a slit either side of the skirt just sew down as far as the slit. To prevent the slit suddenly extending up to the armpits as you dance the night away, backstitch a couple of stitches to secure it.

Run parallel lines of shirring across the bodice section 2cm apart down as far as you wish. You might first sew four lines of shirring over the bust to give the dress an empire line. Hold it against yourself, look in the mirror and if you like it stop shirring. If it doesn't suit you carry on shirring and keep trying the dress against you until you like the effect. Don't forget to fasten all the ends of the shirring properly. Check with page 45 to see how you apply the straps, if you're having any.

If you choose the style with the side slits you must make a double turning and hem each side of the slit. Sew the other side seam up. Double turn the hem 3cm and 5cm, and sew it.

A fancy frill

Add a frill, if you like, along the bottom of the dress before you sew up the second side seam. First double turn and sew a narrow hem along the top and bottom edges of the frill piece. Then sew two parallel rows of big running stitches, the first row 2cm down from the top edge and the second row 3mm below it. Pull these threads to gather up the material until it's short enough to go along the bottom of the skirt. Attach it like this by laying 2cm of the frill over the bottom 2cm of the skirt.

Complete the dress by sewing up the other side seam.

A gathered pocket

The pretty pocket shown on the skirt of the short dress (see page 41) looks square when finished but it starts out as a shape like this:

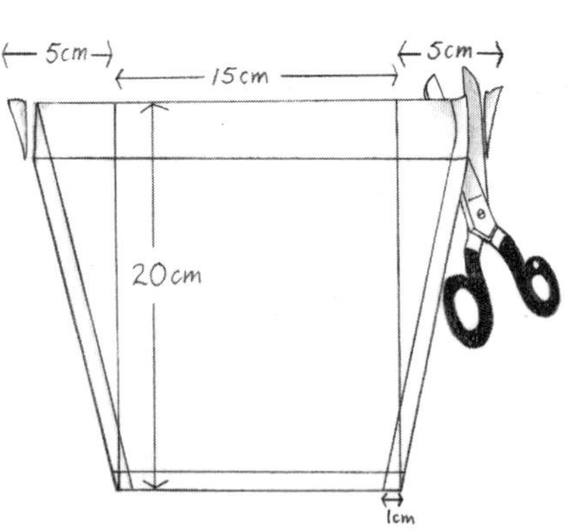

Either draw the shape on a piece of paper, cut it out and use it as a pattern; or draw it in tailor's chalk straight on to your fabric. First draw a rectangle 15 × 20cm. On each end of the top 15cm edge add 5cm. Join each of these two new points to the corners of the old 15cm edge of the rectangle. Measure down 3cm from the top (your turning) and draw a line across. Measure 1cm in on the other three sides for the other turnings. Snip through the turning allowance at the two top corners. Double turn the top edge 5mm and then 2·5cm. Sew it. Run a row of shirring along just under this hem, on the single thickness of fabric, and then a second row, 1cm below. Pin under a 1cm single turning round the three raw edges of the pocket – be careful to catch the top corners down neatly. Pin the pocket to the skirt in the position which is comfortable for you and sew it on.

Making a shirred skirt

On one of the 91cm edges of each of the rectangles of fabric make a mark, both sides, 2·5cm in. Draw a straight line from each of these marks down to the corner below it. Cut off these four narrow triangles. This shapes the skirt in slightly at the waist. With the right sides together sew up one side seam 2cm in. Along the waist edge make a double turning, first 1cm and then 1·5cm. Pin it and sew it. With tailor's chalk and ruler draw your shirring guide-lines (see page 45) with the first one 2cm down from the top edge. The following lines are all spaced 2cm apart.

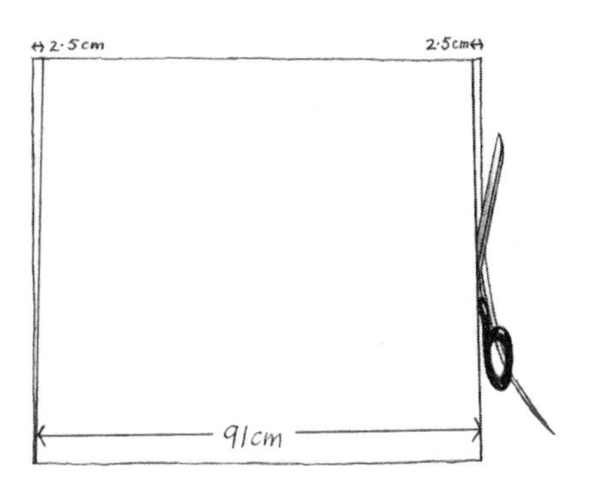

Do four rows of shirring and see how the skirt looks wrapped around you. Depending on your figure, you may like to leave it at that or you may prefer to add a few more rows. Having finished all the shirring sew up the other side seam. Turn the hem under first 2cm and then 5cm and sew it. If you would like a frill along the bottom or pocket the instructions are in the previous section on making a dress.

Some dual-purpose designs

These are some more ideas using shirring, merely outlined but not explained in detail. The technical know-how in the preceding few pages applies here too so do refer back.

A dress-cum-skirt

This is a great dual-purpose garment. As with all shirring, use a lightweight fabric. It makes a pretty daytime summer dress or a long skirt that can be worn at any time of the year. For parties on chilly nights it can conceal a multitude of petticoats, two pairs of socks, boots and woolly long johns.

For an average size – anything from 81cm to 91cm bust – it requires:

Sew one side seam to join the two pieces and one side seam to join the two bottom bits, giving you two long narrow strips. Run four lines of shirring along the top section. Gather the lower strip until it corresponds with the length of the top strip. Sew the bottom to the top strip. Finish off by sewing up the remaining side seam and the hem.

Wear the dress strapless or add a halter-neck strap. When you are wearing the garment as a long skirt just push the strap out of sight inside the waistband.

You could make a dress/skirt like this with many more than just two tiers. This would be particularly suitable if you were recycling something that gave you long narrow strips, like a sheet that's worn out down the centre or odd-shaped curtains with frilly pelmets. What about mixing different patterned fabrics?

Here's a nice touch – ribbon threaded through the bottom tier which is made from an old piece of lace curtain. (It's useful to know that you can cut a piece of lace to give you a fancy edge by cutting closely round the actual motifs.)

A short nightie-cum-summer-top

This is made in the same way as the dresses previously described except that the shirring rows are spaced differently. The top row is 2cm down from the top edge. Then there is a second row 1cm below it. This is followed by a gap of 9cm of plain fabric and then three rows of shirring again spaced 1cm apart. The depth of the unshirred fabric over the bust (suggested here as 9cm) depends on how well you are endowed bust-wise. So adjust the space between the two areas of shirring to suit your figure.

Magic rectangles

It's so easy – it seems too good to be true. From a small heap of rectangles of material you can make all these clothes. All you have to do is to lace the rectangles together (as you lace up your shoes) in different arrangements to make different garments. The great advantage is that you can then just unlace them and re-assemble them to make something new.

You need various numbers of rectangles for the different garments. For example, for a tabard you'll need four rectangles; for a medium-length dress, ten. Each rectangle is the same size: 54 × 27cm (a double square).

None of these garments is intended to be tight-fitting and this size of rectangle will fit anyone around average size. However, if you are exceptionally small or rather large you may have to adjust the size of the rectangles. Measure and cut some 54 × 27cm rectangles out of newspaper. Hold them around and against you to see if any adjustment is necessary.

The most suitable kind of fabric is something of the weight of a heavyish tweed, elephant corduroy (that's the one with big fat lines across it) or quilted material. Now, it's extremely unlikely that you'll be able to lay your hands on enough material to cut out ten rectangles all 54 × 27cm. Even four might present a problem. A great solution is to use patchwork and make the rectangles up out of smaller pieces. Patchwork looks fabulous for this project because you can combine your patchworked rectangles in all sorts of clever ways.

To end up with rectangles of the right weight use any of these three methods: patches cut from tweeds and fabrics of a comparable thickness (see page 120); patchworked knitted pieces (details on page 128); or a quilted cotton patchwork (page 136). You can make your rectangles up using one or all of the various techniques.

IMPORTANT. *Thick, soft quilting, such as that you make using bought synthetic wadding, ends up smaller all round than when you started. So, in this case, you must allow some extra fabric. Trim the rectangles to the right size after you have finished all the quilting.*

Each 54 × 27cm rectangle divides up nicely into eight squares, each 13·5 × 13·5cm when sewn. As the outside edges of the completed rectangle are to be bound you do not need the usual turning allowance of 1·5cm on each side of each square. So the pieces are cut out like this before you sew them together:

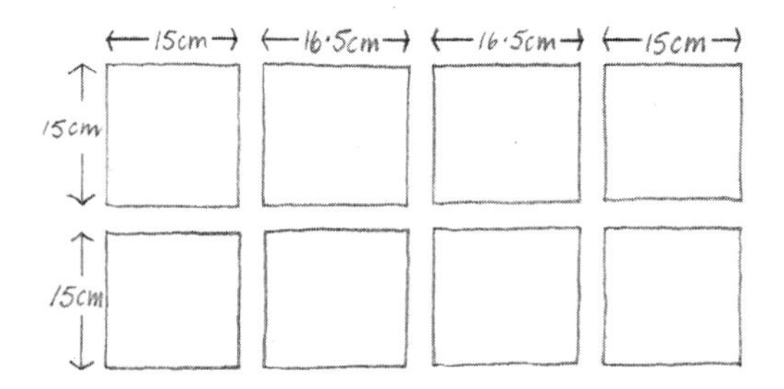

Four rectangles which, when finally sewn, each measure 13·5 × 27cm could be arranged like this (these are the sizes you should cut out):

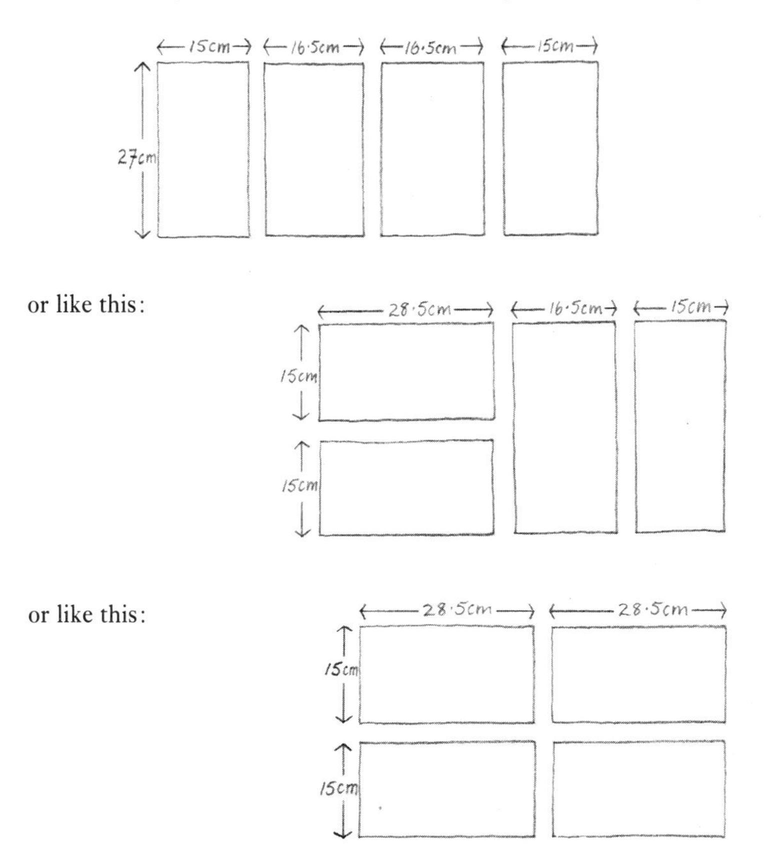

or like this:

or like this:

Crazy patchwork would be super too.

Unless a lining is an integral part of the patchwork technique you are using you should line the rectangles. (Jumble sale curtain linings will be useful here.)

Whichever way you patchwork your rectangles, finish up by binding the edges. This gives an attractive finish and a good firm support for the lacing. Have 2cm of the binding showing on the front and 2cm on the back. If you're using braid or something similar to cover and secure the joins on your patchwork use this same braid (or a wider version of it) for the edging. In other cases bind with webbing, tape or home-made binding strips (explained on page 124). The final thickness of the rectangle, with its lining and possibly quilting, dictates how wide the binding strips should be cut. Experiment by measuring and folding a piece of paper round to find the correct width, including the turnings.

Different ways of lacing

You can either make holes or loops to thread the laces through to join one rectangle to another.

Eyelet holes

For hole-making you can buy a tool to fit metal eyelets. You can get it either at a craft shop or from the sewing-aids stand in most chain stores or supermarkets. With one type you have to bash the metal eyelet into the fabric with a hammer. It's all explained on the pack and is not at all difficult. Another kind, which is a little more expensive, looks like a pair of pliers. If you have trouble buying eyelets in quantity, contact Dryad Ltd (page 185).

If you prefer it, you can sew eyelet holes, like tiny little buttonholes. Punch out the hole with something sharp that's the right size – a prong of the carving fork perhaps–and blanket stitch all round the edges.

Measure out and mark the position of each eyelet with a dot in pencil or tailor's chalk. On the 54 × 27cm rectangle, in order to be spaced evenly to match up in all directions, they go as follows:

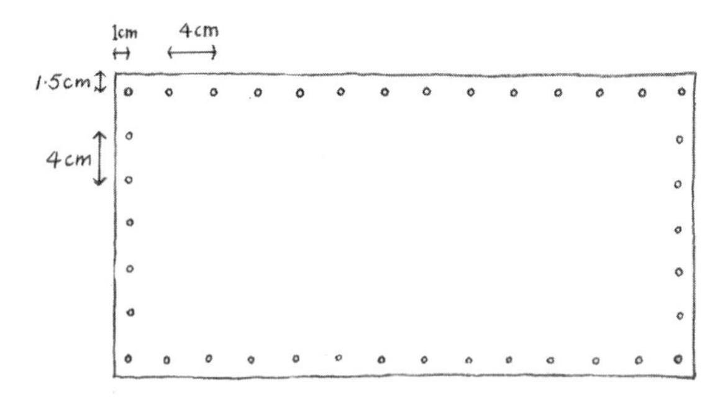

On the long sides of the rectangle they are 1·5cm in from the edge and spaced out every 4cm. On the short sides they are 1cm in from the edge and also 4cm apart. If you are changing the size of the rectangle you must carefully work out the even distribution of the eyelet points to fit into your new measurements. The eyelets must be the same distance apart along each edge.

Loops

Here is how to make loops for the lacing up instead of eyelets. You'll need some narrow tape, sometimes called seam binding, or straight tape in a suitable colour. Mark out the points where the loops will go in exactly the same way as for the eyelets. Cut little bits of tape, 3·5cm long, one for each loop. Fold each piece of tape in half and pin it on to the binding at the back of the rectangle at the appropriate point. The ones at the corners go on diagonally. Run a double line of stitching along to fasten all the loops on securely. (If hand sewing use backstitch.)

You could also make the loops from russia braid, which is a narrow double-cord kind of braid. This comes in a range of lovely colours and is surprisingly cheap. It does unravel easily so be careful to sew the loops on very, very thoroughly.

Lacing up

Lace the rectangles together with a ribbon or cord that suits the type of materials you have used. Baby-blue satin ribbon might look a bit silly on a patchwork of suedette all in different dark browns. Bright scarlet russia braid would be much more in keeping, or lengths of leather bootlace. (It's also wise to have a lace that's thin enough to go through the holes!) You can buy leather bootlacing by the metre from some cobblers and craft shops. It's quite cheap. Because russia braid and similar braids and cords tend to fray when you cut them, you may have a big problem with threading up. Here's how to get round it. Cut the ends so that they are nice and neat. Dip them in nail varnish to a depth of 1·5cm. Hang them up, and when they are dry you'll have excellent rigid threading ends.

A wrap-around skirt

You can make this skirt from any large flat piece of fabric. It has a really simple tie fastening – no zips or anything. The waistband and the fastenings are all in one. The skirt can be short or long and, being cut from a half circle, it hangs in a rather nice sexy way.

For a summer version tie and dye an old sheet, bedspread or tablecloth. Or make an old bath towel into a wrap-around and then you'll have not only a skirt but a useful cover-up for the beach – fine to undress under if you're modest. Make a really short one as a super sports skirt.

For winter, convert an unwanted blanket (tartan would be great) but don't use too thick a material, as it won't hang properly. Or make up a piece of patchwork with giant squares of tweed or woollen fabrics. Crazy patchwork (see page 120) is another idea – or a denim patchwork.

First you must establish that you have a big enough piece of material. To do this measure your waist and write it down on a piece of paper. Add on 15cm, which is the wrap-over. Divide this figure by 3. This gives you the radius of the curve to fit round your waist. Now measure and write down the length you want the skirt to be. Add on 2·5cm for turnings. Here, for example, the waist measures 60cm, the length 64cm. Your skirt will be cut from a rectangle folded in half to make two equal squares. The total of your sum gives you the length of the side of the square. So for our example the piece of fabric for the skirt must be at least 91·5 × 183cm. Then you must have enough fabric for the waistband. If you can't cut it out all in one piece it can be joined.

The waistband is 8cm deep and you calculate the length like this:

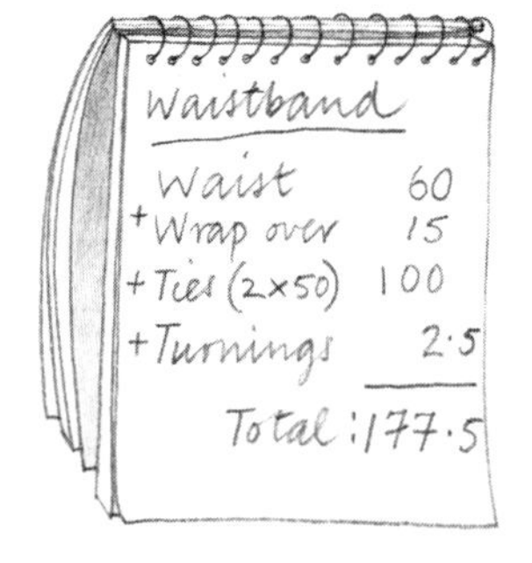

Remember this is only a fictitious example. You will be using your own waist measurement.

Here are four versions of this easily made wrap-around skirt.

Now you will need something with which to draw on the fabric – chalk if a pencil won't show – a drawing-pin, a length of string, scissors, your sewing gear and the iron.

Having done your sums, iron the material and fold it in half, wrong side out. It may be easiest to work on the floor but do make sure the dog doesn't wander in all over everything.

Tie the pencil or chalk to one end of the string. Along the string measure the length which is your waist measurement, plus 15cm for the wrap-over, divided by 3 – in this example 25cm. Push the drawing-pin through the string at that point and through the top, folded, left-hand corner of the fabric. Keeping the string stretched tight draw a quarter of a circle. Remove the drawing-pin and replace it through the string at a length which is the sum of the waist measurement, plus the wrap-over, divided by 3 + the skirt length + 2·5cm for turnings. So in our example it is 91·5cm.

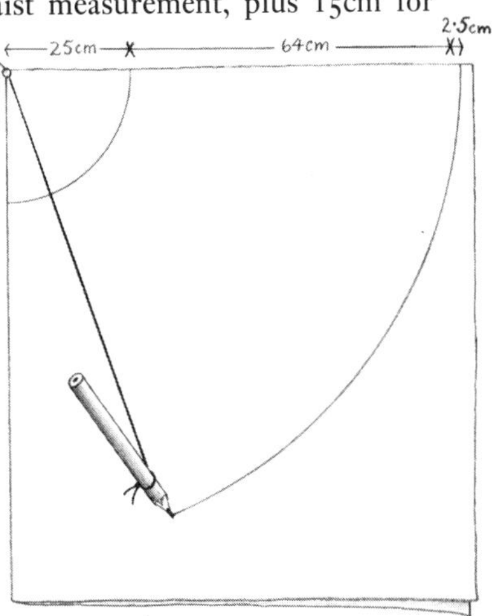

Drawing-pin in the corner again and draw out the big curve. Cut this shape out. When you open it out you will have this shape.

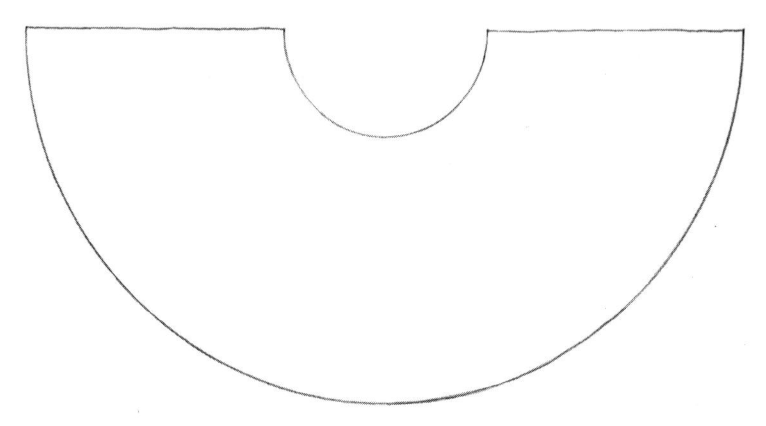

Double turn and hem the two straight side seams.

Cut out the waistband (along the grain of the fabric, that is, parallel with the selvedge), joining pieces if necessary. Fold the long strip in half lengthwise, wrong side out. Pin it to stop it wobbling about. From each end measure in 52cm and mark these two points. Except for the folded long side and the gap between the two 52cm marks sew all the way round the waistband, about 1cm in. Make little (careful) cuts upwards where the stitching ends. Don't cut through the stitches.

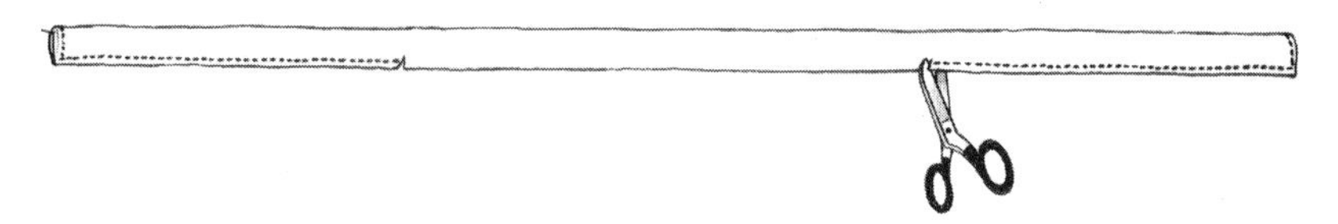

Turn this inside out so that the right side is now facing outwards. With a pin pull out the corners so that they are nice and sharp. You now have a sausage with an undercarriage like this:

Fold one of the loose lower pieces under and iron it down so that it continues the line of the sewn edge. To attach the waistband to the skirt lay the skirt piece out wrong side up and pin the flapping, unsewn bit of the waistband to it (right side of waistband on to wrong side of skirt).

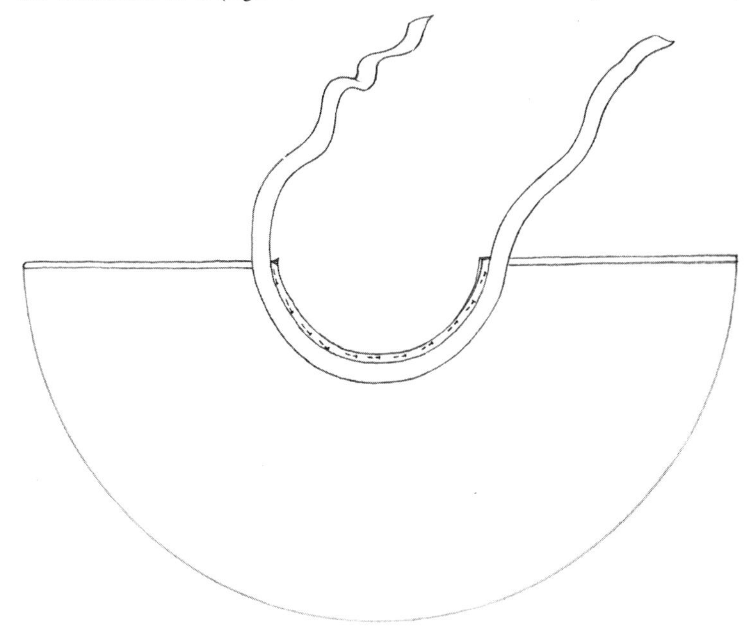

Sew round this 1cm in. Lay the skirt out right side up and pin on the other side of the unsewn section of the waistband with the ironed turning lying nicely inside. Arrange it so that it covers over the previous line of stitching. Sew this side on either with machine or hemming stitch.

For the ties to fasten neatly when you are wearing the skirt one tie has to actually pass through the waistband. So from the right-hand edge of the skirt (i.e. the side seam) measure 30cm in along the waistband. Pinch the waistband and cut a tiny slit which when opened out will be wide enough for the tie to pass through. Blanket stitch round the edge of this to stop it fraying, making the stitches really close together (see page 21).

If yours is a patchwork skirt, especially denim, you may like to fray the bottom edge instead of hemming it. Otherwise turn the edge under twice, making a narrow hem and sew it. Iron it all and the skirt is finished.

You can wear it with the overlap and the ties fastened in whichever position you like, at the front, the back or the side.

Happiness is a happi coat

This easy-to-make-coat is based on the Japanese kimono style. Make it in a lightweight material as a summer wrap for the beach or for general lounging about. You could recycle a sheet or some curtains or a large tablecloth. The photograph shows a happi coat made from a plain white sheet.

Made up in a heavier fabric it becomes a warm winter coat or a cosy dressing-gown. Use an old blanket or make it from a patchwork of tweeds, heavy corduroys, etc. It can be full- or calf-length or just down to your bottom for a jacket. Happi coats are fine for men too.

With the exception of the front cross-over all the pieces are rectangles.

The tie belt can be literally a tie – a man's tie made in an attractive fabric (easily procured at a jumble sale) or a long scarf, a piece of wide ribbon or a wide belt made in the same fabric as the coat itself.

Start off by writing your own measurements in on the dotted lines of this diagram:

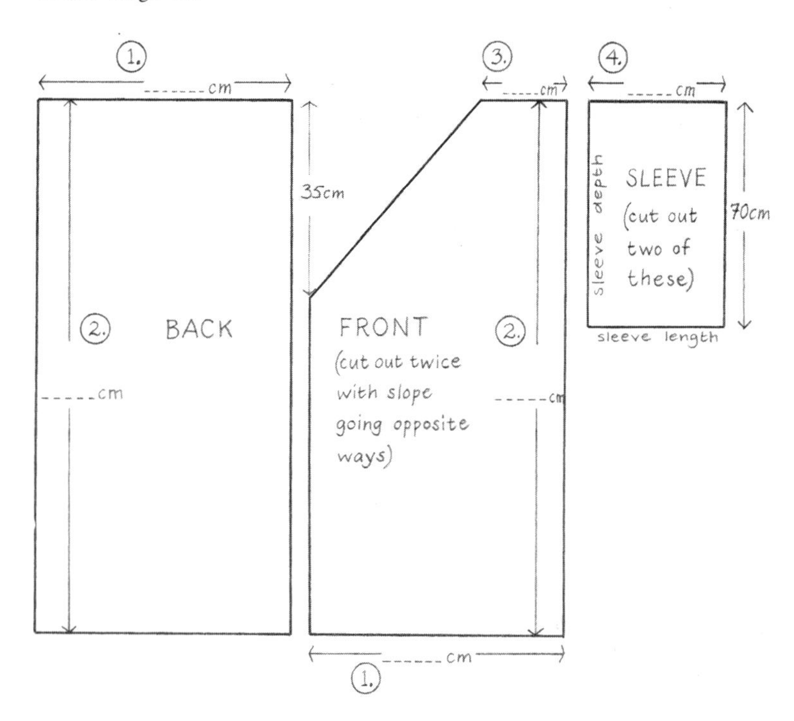

The same pattern, but two totally different coats. Her housecoat is made from an old sheet; his technicolour jacket was a jumble-sale crazy-patchwork quilt.

1. Measure round your bust (or a man's chest). Divide this measurement by two. To the answer add 10cm, that is, 5cm each side, as the garment is not supposed to be close-fitting. Fill in the two spaces on the diagram marked (1).

2. To find the length measure down from the nape of the neck to where you want the hemline to be. Add on 4cm for turnings and complete the two (2) spaces.

3. Measure from where your neck joins your shoulder out to the bone at the outside edge of your shoulder. Add on 5cm. Fill in space (3).

4. The sleeve depth is 70cm (including turnings). It is folded in half, the seam being underneath. Calculate your own sleeve length by measuring from the outer end of measurement (3) down along the outside of your crooked arm to wherever you want the sleeve to finish and add 4cm for turnings. Fill in space (4). The sleeves in the photographs are 37cm long.

Imagine the front piece as a rectangle exactly the same size as the back piece. To work out the angle of the slope first measure down 35cm on one side, i.e. the depth of the sleeve when folded in half. Join this 35cm point with a straight line to the inner end (neck) of measurement (3).

Lay your fabric (nicely ironed) out on the floor and with tailor's chalk, a set square and a ruler draw out the shapes according to your measurements. The set square is to make proper right angles. These are important. If you haven't got a set square use the corner of a piece of paper from an old exercise book or magazine. Draw the two front pieces out first as rectangles and then add the sloping lines. How you cut out those shapes that occur twice (the fronts and the sleeves) depends upon the shape of the fabric you are using. If you are recycling something rather an odd shape you will have to fit the pieces in wherever you can and cut each one out individually. However, if you are able to cut out the sleeves and fronts in one go through two thicknesses of fabric do make sure that you put the right sides of the cloth together. If not, you'll end up with two right-hand fronts – un-happi.

Having cut out all the pieces pin and sew the shoulder seams first, right sides together. Sew all seams 2cm in. Press seams flat.

Fold the sleeve in half to find the middle of the top edge. Mark this point with a pin. Sew the sleeves on, with the marked point lined up with the shoulder seam. Press these seams.

Now sew up the sleeve seams and the two side seams, leaving slits at the bottom of the latter. Be careful to secure the sewing at the end of each slit with a few backstitches. The length of the side slits is your choice. Those in the photographs are 25cm long.

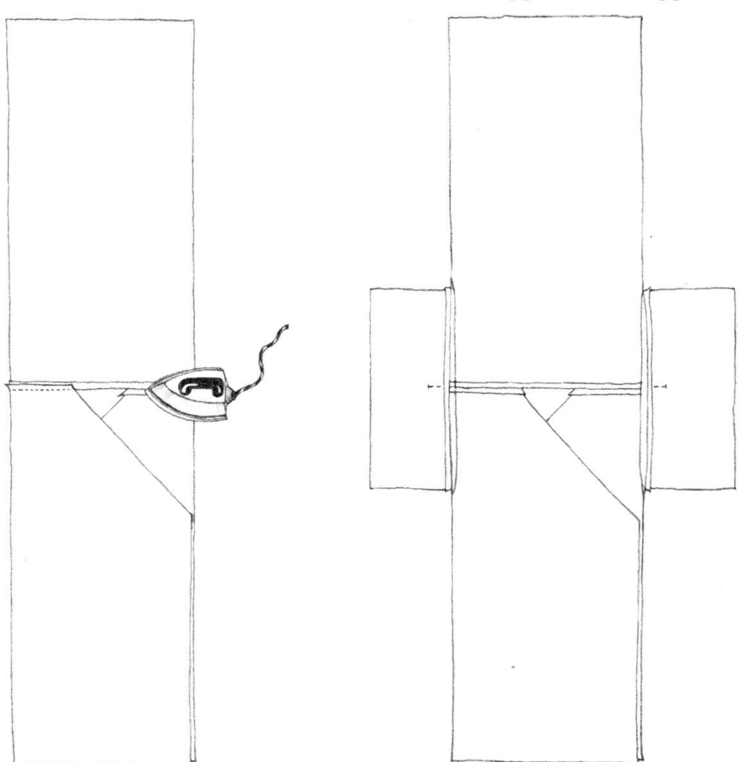

Double turn the hem right round the neck opening – along one slope, round the back of the neck and down the other slope. To make the actual neck part turn under neatly make little cuts in the seam allowance at the corners.

Double turn and hem the ends of the sleeves. Double turn and hem the edges of the slits and the bottom hemline. Tidy up any rough edges inside by pinking or oversewing.

On the bottom point of the slope of the left front sew a popper to link up with its other half, which you sew on the side seam just under the sleeve. On a man's coat the popper should be on the right front.

Work out where you want your belt to tie. It could be at the centre back or at the side. Sew it to the right front piece at the bottom of the slope so that appropriate lengths are left to tie wherever you want them to.

A versatile top

This elementary idiot-proof pattern can be made up into a range of tops for a variety of occasions.

It's the same pattern – but in different materials it looks a totally different garment. The basics are two identical front and back pieces plus two stretchy cuffs and a stretchy waistband.

For a sports top – après tennis or swimming – make it from a couple of hand towels. A slinky party top can be made in silk or chiffon. Make a

Tie-and-dye sample pieces have been sewn together to make this version of the top.

cosy woolly sweater out of knitted or crocheted squares sewn together. For a lighter top, recycle a straight, boring, aunt-like dress made in, say, acrylic jersey fabric.

The waistband and cuffs can be cut off an unwanted sweater – or sweaters. It might be rather fun to have one red cuff and one green one, and a purple waistband: or you can use elasticated webbing which you buy at a haberdasher's (nice subtle colours). Sew it into the appropriate-sized tubes (i.e. ones that fit comfortably round you) before you attach it to the top. Another idea is to make your own cuff and waistband by shirring some lengths of fabric (details on shirring on page 44). Or what about knitting your own bits of ribbing?

As the front and the back pieces of the garment are the same shape cut one pattern out of a large sheet of newspaper. Fold the paper in half. The fold represents the vertical centre front or centre back. Measure from the nape of the neck along the outside of the shoulder and bent arm (as shown on page 35) to the wrist, or higher up the arm if you want shorter sleeves. At the top of the paper draw this measurement as a straight line at a right angle to the fold. Then measure from the nape down to your waist. Add on 15cm to allow for easy movement. This is the depth of your garment so measure it down the fold from the top line and make a mark at this point.

Now take your waist measurement and divide it by 4. From the depth measurement point, again at a right angle to the fold, draw a line a quarter of your waist measurement long plus 20cm. (This will all be gathered into the waistband.) With your ruler join up the end of this waistband line to the end of the top outer sleeve line. This gives you the pattern shape. Cut out the paper shape and then the two fabric pieces.

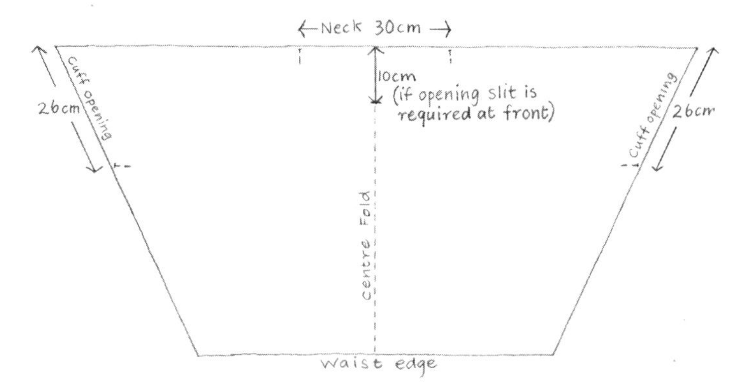

With soft, stretchy knitted fabrics you can leave the front of the neck opening as a straight line. However, with stiffer fabrics it is necessary to introduce a centre slit to avoid choking. On the paper pattern mark, on the fold, a point 10cm down from the top edge. Open out the pattern, pin it to the fabric piece and, cutting through paper and fabric together, cut the slit (on the front only). Remove the paper pattern.

Put pin markers 15cm either side of the slit, or, if it is the style without a slit, either side of the centre front. Sew the outer sleeve seams 1·5cm in from the pin markers to the end of the straight edge.

For the cuff openings measure and pin mark 26cm down from the top outside corners. From these markers sew the side seams (1·5cm in) right down to the bottom.

Finish the edges of the neck hole and slit with zigzag or hand over-sewing. Then sew a single hem.

Attach each ribbed tube section by stretching and pinning it so that it is pulled out to fill the hole that's been left for it. When you let go the ribbing will contract and automatically gather up the fabric. Sew the ribbing and the fabric together 1·5cm in.

On the sports top the outer sleeve seams are bound in coloured tape (maybe in your club colours) before they are sewn together. For binding details see page 124. If you have a zigzagging machine use this to join the bound outer sleeve seams. If not, turn the garment inside out and carefully oversew the two pieces together. The stitches should be invisible on the right side.

Cape ability

Sick of your old winter coat? No money to buy a fashionable new one? Aghast and horrified at the prospect of making one? If you are looking for a cheap way to keep warm in winter make an easy-to-sew cape. Even the dumbest dressmaker is cape-able.

Wear your cape successfully with any outfit from jeans and sweater to evening dress. If icy winds blow you can pile on the jumpers, top them with your cape and still look stylish whilst the cape-less go round looking like Michelin men. A cape looks good on a fellow too.

To make a full-length cape you will need either a double blanket or a piece of warm material that sort of size, i.e. 228 × 254cm. You might get a blanket or an old chenille tablecover in a jumble sale; or perhaps a kind auntie will take pity on poor freezing you and give you one that is a bit worn out. You can always patch it in a decorative way (see page 170). Another idea is to make up a big flat piece of patchwork from old woollen skirts, coats and jackets. Middle-aged type skirts and men's tweed jackets are generally ignored at jumbles and they are often made from super fabrics.

The basic cape shape is a half circle – just as in the wrap-around skirt on page 56. Depending on how long you want your cape to be, you will require a piece of fabric out of which a shape like this can be cut:

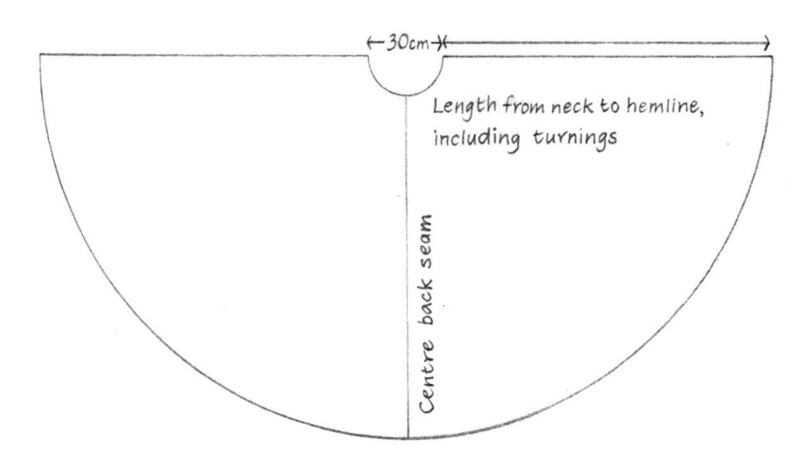

Ask someone to measure you from where your neck meets your shoulder, over the shoulder and down the arm (held straight) to the ankle or whatever length you fancy. To this measurement add 15cm for the neck hole and 2·5cm for turnings.

Iron the material. Now you'll need a ruler, a pencil, a pair of compasses, some paper (newspaper will do) a drawing-pin, some string, a stick of chalk, scissors, some thick wool in a contrasting colour, your sewing equipment and a spare floor where you can spread everything out.

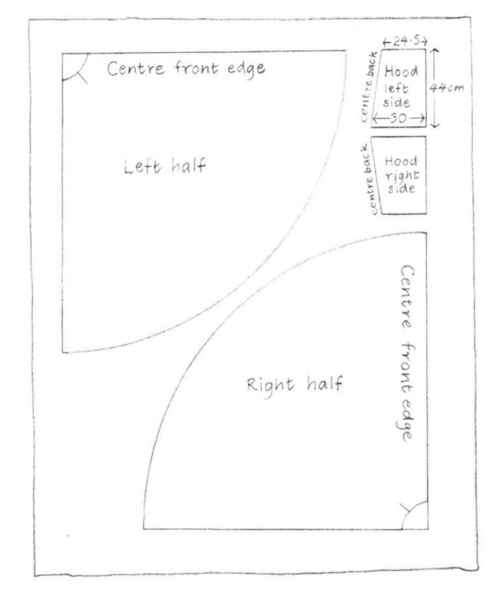

Lay the fabric out flat with the wrong side up. The two halves of the cape and the two halves of the hood will be arranged as in the sketch on the left.

To draw the big arc tie the chalk to the string. From the chalk measure along the string the length of your cape + 15cm + 2·5cm. At this point poke the drawing-pin through the string. Stick the drawing-pin in the top left-hand corner of the fabric and draw a big arc with the string stretched taut. Now draw another identical arc in the diagonally opposite corner.

Make a simple paper pattern for the neck hole. Set your compasses to a radius of 15cm. Place the point in the corner of the paper and draw a quarter circle. Now you have to adjust the shape of the neck hole. The way your body is made means that a neck opening must be lower at the front than at the back. If you made your cape with an even semicircular neck it would gape at the back and probably strangle you at the front.

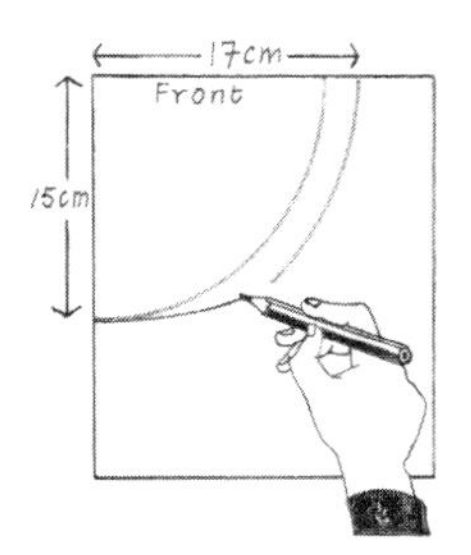

Re-set the compasses to radius 17cm. With the point in the same place as before draw the new wider arc just half-way round the outside of the first. Then, drawing freehand, draw a curve that makes the wider arc merge into the smaller one. Write 'FRONT' along the longer edge. Cut this paper shape out.

Place the paper pattern in the corner of the fabric within the wide arc. Chalk round it and chalk an F for 'front' on the appropriate straight edge. Do the same in the other cape half.

Draw the hood shape twice (two sides) on the fabric. This is a wonky rectangle. Along a right-angled corner on the material measure out and mark 24·5cm in one direction, and 44cm in the other direction. At a right angle to this longer measurement draw another line 30cm long. Join the end of the 30cm line to the 24·5cm mark at a slope.

The cape has to be slightly shaped in order to fit comfortably on your shoulders. This is achieved by taking a dart on each shoulder. Fold your paper pattern in half, straight sides together. Open the paper out and fit it inside the chalked neck-hole shape on the fabric. Lay the ruler along the fold line and, out beyond the paper shape, chalk a line 10cm long. Either side of this line, along the curved line, mark 1·8cm from the line. Join these marks to the outer end of the 10cm line, making a long narrow triangle. Do the same in the other half of the cape.

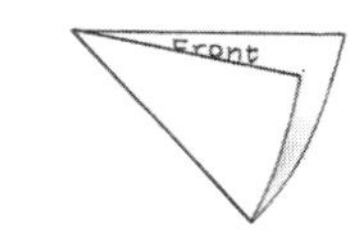

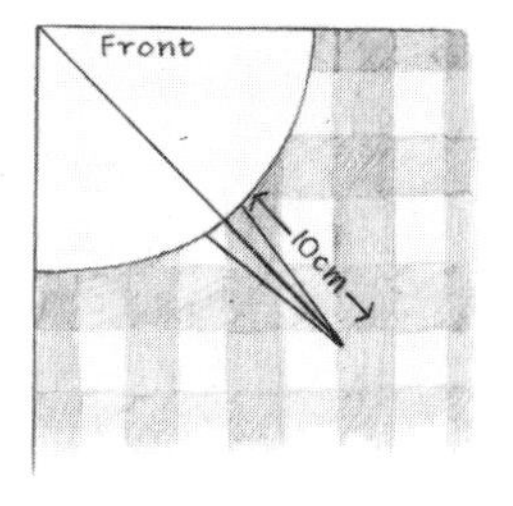

Now cut the four pieces out of the fabric, but don't cut into the darts. First do the darts. On the wrong side of the fabric fold along the 10cm line, lining up the outside points of the base of the long narrow triangle. Pin this triangular tuck along the chalked lines (the outside edges of the triangle) and then sew it. Now sew the two halves of the cape together 2cm in along the centre-back seam, right sides together. Along the two centre-front edges fold under a double turning of first 1cm and then 2cm and sew.

Sew the centre-back seam of the hood 1cm in and then the top of the hood, also 1cm in.

Lay the cape out flat, right side up. Lay the hood on top, wrong side out with its centre-back seam lying on top of the cape's centre-back seam. Put a pin through the hood and the cape, joining them at the two centre seams. Work your way round to the left, pinning the hood to the cape. Do the same to the right. The hood will extend some 2cm beyond the

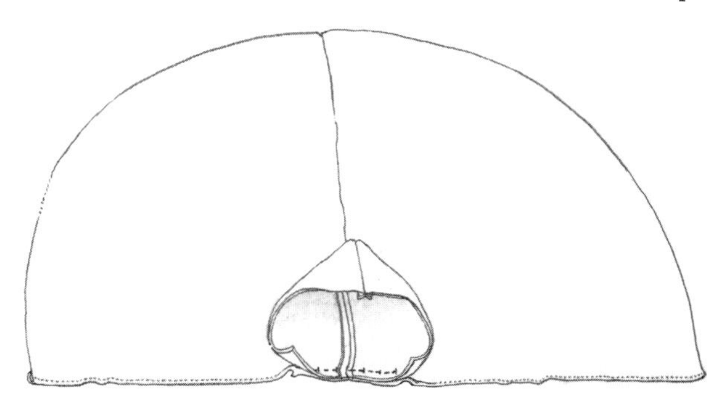

cape. Remove the two extreme outside pins on either side. Make a double turning along the edge of the hood. This is the front edge from which your face will look out. This turning should be about 2cm but adjust it if necessary so that the front edge of the hood lines up with the front edge of the cape.

Having sewn the hood edge turning, replace those outside pins. Tack the hood to the cape, flattening out seams and darts as you come to them. Sew the hood and cape together 1·5cm in.

The cape fastens at the neck. Make two plaits of wool about the thickness of a pencil and 28cm long. Finish them like a girl's pigtails by binding some wool round, leaving a little brush about 3cm long. Or finish them off with woolly bobbles (see how to make them on page 29). Sew the plaits on at the front, where the hood and the cape join, to tie in a bow under your chin. For a masculine version of the cape choose one of the methods of fastening explained on page 25.

With the wool (double if necessary) go over the seams inside the hood with big, bold blanket stitches in either a matching or contrasting colour. These seams show when you wear the cape with the hood hanging down at the back. In the same way blanket stitch round the neck seam. If your material is very inclined to fray you will have to make a small double turning round the hemline (rather a long journey). If it's not a very fraying fabric you can blanket stitch the unturned edge. A cape made in a patterned or textured cloth is complete now. However, if your fabric is a bit dull, as an ordinary cream blanket may be, cheer it up by adding blanket stitch along the front edge of the hood and down the two centre fronts. For fun you could alternate 12cm of blue blanket stitch with 12cm of red. A strip of fur or fur fabric would look fabulous edging the hood. Keep your eyes open – you might find some. You could always add it later.

A waistcoat – or a gilet, if you're feeling rather French

This super boxy waistcoat is made entirely from rectangular pieces. This means there are no complicated corners to sew; also you can use up small pieces of fabric or bits cut out of other items. The waistcoat can be unlined or lined. If the latter, you can make it reversible – two waistcoats in one. The girl in the photos is wearing a reversible waistcoat. One side is made from the left-over pieces of the blanket that was used to make the cape on page 67. On the reverse side the back panel is part of a jumble-purchased embroidered cushion cover; the other sections are cut from a jumble velvet cocktail dress. (This proved a very good two pence worth, as it also had some handy black lace on it.)

Suitable fabrics are tweed, quilted material, woollies patchwork (page 128), fur fabric – fabulous, watch out for remnants – suede or leather (if you can get them). The boy's waistcoat is made from a lightweight carpet remnant.

The dimensions given here will fit anyone with a bust or chest measurement from 86cm to 96cm. You can make the waistcoat up with the two centre-front pieces and ties or without them as an open-fronted little number. The measurements have a 1·5cm seam allowance all round. If your waistcoat is to be lined cut out exactly the same pieces in the lining material too. If you are going to make a bound version, like the one the girl is wearing in the photo, knock off 1·5cm all the way round, as there will be no turnings. These are the pieces:

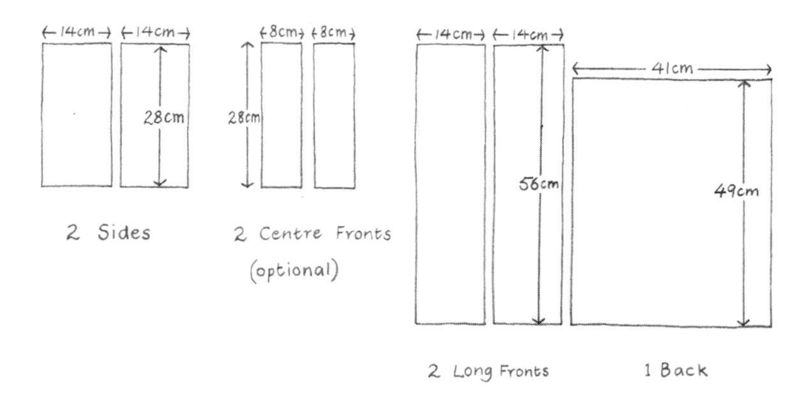

You can go ahead and draw these straight on to the fabric and cut them out.

Coffee

To make the waistcoat in a size outside the 86cm to 96cm range adjust the pattern by altering the sizes or proportions of the rectangles. There are no funny angles or curves to worry about. The simplest thing is to enlarge or decrease the width of the side pieces. Cut out the new-size rectangles in newspaper, pin them together and, with extreme care and some contortions, try on the paper waistcoat. This will show you if it needs any further adjustment.

The 'with binding' style

To make the bound-edges version without the two centre fronts, you'll need 6·25 metres of binding (for the size given here). The centre fronts take an extra 1·5 metres and, if you are having six ties, get another 1·5 metres – 25cm per tie – so that's 9·25 metres in all.

For a lined or reversible waistcoat lay each outer fabric piece exactly on top of its corresponding inner piece. Pin the two pieces together, not too near the edge or the pins will get mixed up with the binding. Now treat the double layer as a single fabric. First of all bind each rectangular piece all the way round. Easy methods of binding rectangles with strips of fabric or with braid are explained on page 124. Machine zigzagging is the easiest way to join two bound pieces together. Just lay them edge to edge and zigzag across the two. Alternatively, working on the wrong side of the waistcoat, oversew the bound edges together by hand. The stitches shouldn't show on the right side. Another idea – use a decorative embroidery stitch.

If you are having ties pin them on before you bind the centre-front edge. Put the right side of the tie (if it has a right side) to the right side of the fabric so that it appears to be pointing the wrong way, like this:

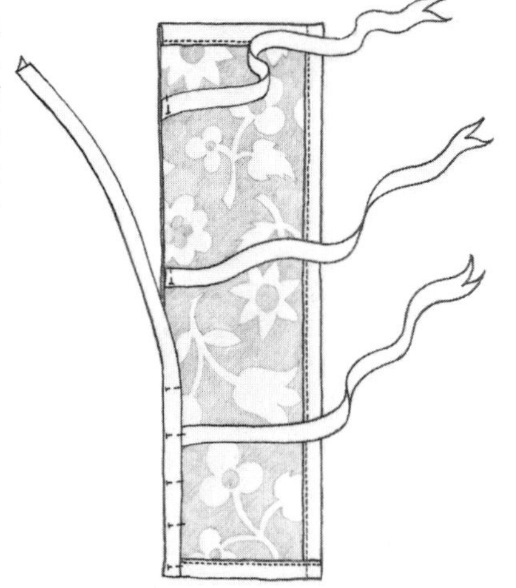

Then put your binding on, and, before the final sewing, fold the tie back into its correct position so that it gets sewn over along with the binding.

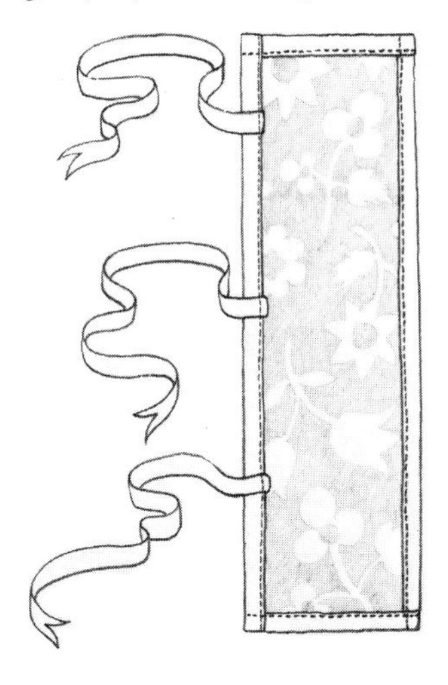

The 'no binding' style

For the style without binding first hem the edges marked with a wiggly line.

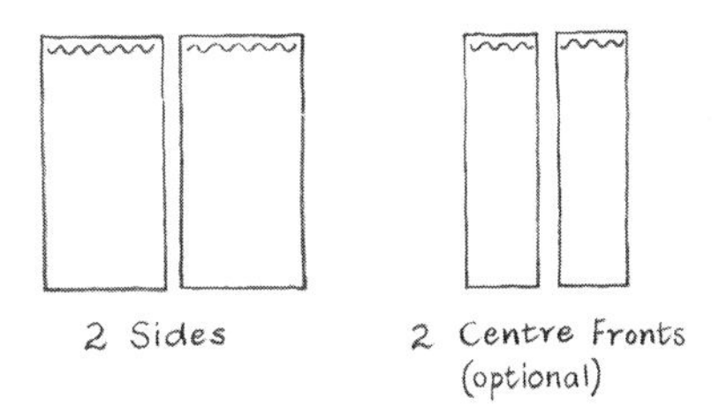

Doing this now avoids tricky corners later. There are different approaches to the hemming, depending on the type of material being used. Avoid a double turning on thick fabrics. With these, finish the raw edge first by zigzagging or oversewing and then turn and sew a single 1·5cm hem. With some fabrics, denim, for example, why not make life simple and just fray the bottom edges?

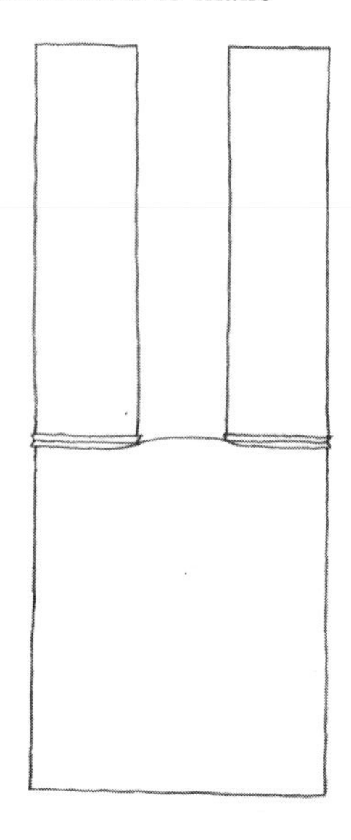

You now have all your rectangles ready – so it's just a case of joining them together. First sew the two long fronts to the back piece.

Then attach the sides, and if you're having them, the centre fronts. Turn and hem all round the neck edge, over the shoulders and round the bottom edge.

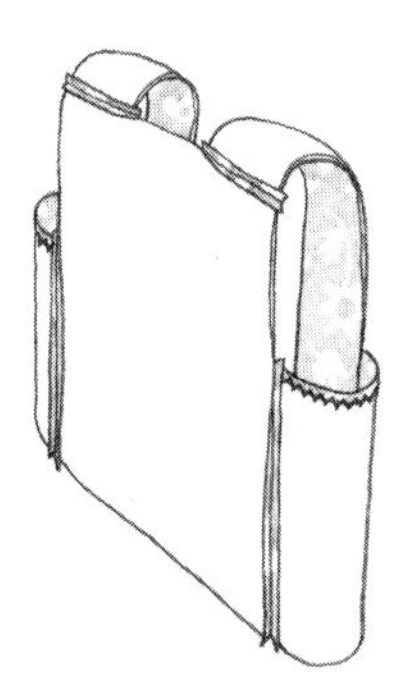

Lined

This is how to make a lined 'no binding' waistcoat. First pin the fabric of each rectangle to its lining, right sides together. Sew 1·5cm in around the two sides and the top. Turn this bag shape inside out so that the right sides come to the outside. Carefully push the corners out with a pencil or something. Press the piece flat and iron under a single 1·5cm turning on the unsewn bottom edge. Now hem along that edge. Sew the rectangles together as for the unlined version.

Have a look at page 24 for some other ideas on fastenings. And there's no reason why your gilet shouldn't have patch pockets too – anywhere you fancy.

Bikini

This simple-to-make cotton bikini adjusts in all directions so it fits virtually any size. Recycle a gingham curtain or tablecloth; use an old cotton dress, a nightie or a shirt. The bikini is lined throughout and you can line it with the same material as the outside, or, if you haven't enough of that, use some other suitable lightweight cotton.

Garments to make

Here's how much material you will need – so you can see if it will come out of that old dress or not.

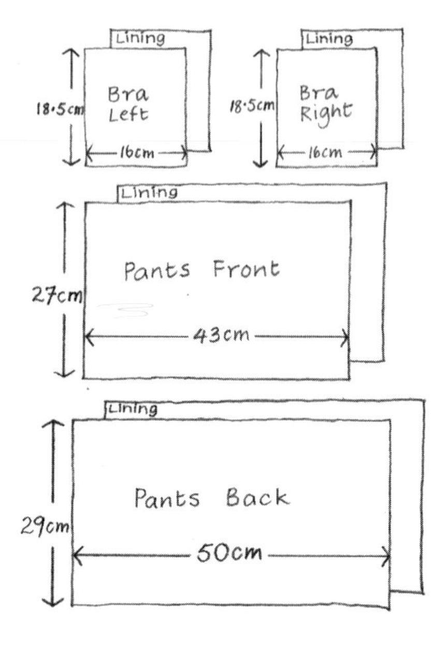

You will also need some narrow 5mm wide elastic: two pieces 40cm long, one bit 33cm and one 24cm; four ordinary shoelaces for the pants ties and two football boot laces for the bra.

The pattern

First of all you have to draw the pattern out on paper – newspaper will do – so you'll need three pieces of paper the sizes given above, one each for the pants front, the pants back and the bra piece. Also have ready a ruler, pencil and set square.

Start with the pants back. Fold the paper in half so it's practically a square. With any symmetrical shape (that means when one half is exactly the same as the other) you only need draw one half. From the folded corner measure 6·5cm along the bottom edge. That's point A. From the right-hand top corner measure down 6·5cm, which is B. Join A to B. From the same right-hand top corner measure in 1·5cm – point C. Join B to C. AB fits around your bottom and (understandably) needs to be slightly curved. Mark the centre of AB, which is 15cm along.

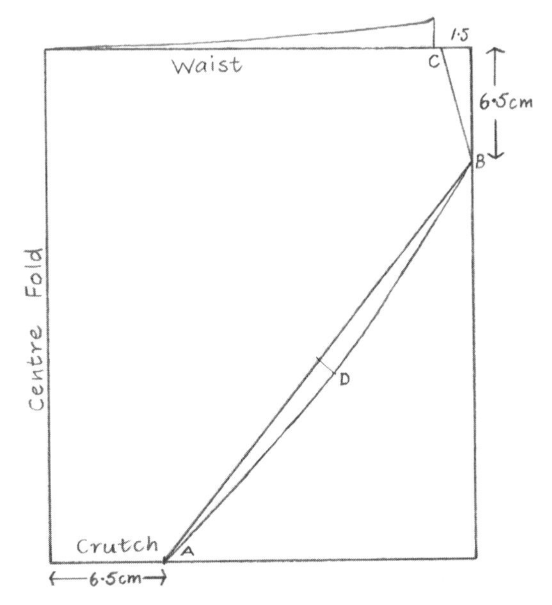

Measure 1cm out to point D. Now, freehand, draw a slight curve from A through D to B. It doesn't matter if you have several goes at it. Carefully cut this shape out. It opens out to look like this:

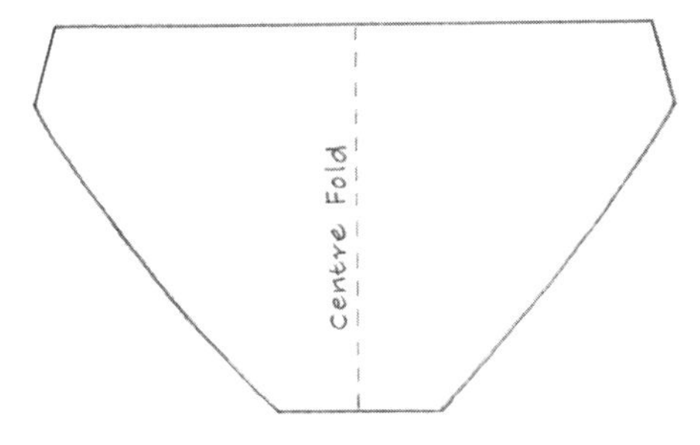

For the pants front fold the paper in half. Measure in 6·5cm from the left-hand bottom corner to point A (the crutch). B is 6cm down this time and C is 1cm in from the corner. Join B to C. On this front part of the pants, AB has to wrap around your thigh, so this is how to work out the curve. It sounds a bit complicated, but just go slowly through it. Along the fold of the paper, starting at the bottom measure upwards 5cm and mark a point called D. Then do this twice again, so that you have three marks in all, D, E and F, each 5cm apart. Make the last mark, G, only 3cm above F. Now draw lines with your set square, to be sure they are at right angles to the fold, across the paper from D, E, F and G. Measure 5cm along the line from D and mark H. From E measure along 5·5cm and mark I. From F measure along 9·5cm and mark J and, finally, from G measure 13·5cm along and mark K.

To get the curve you have, freehand, to join up A, H, I, J, K, and B. Never mind the wobbles – you'll manage it in the end.

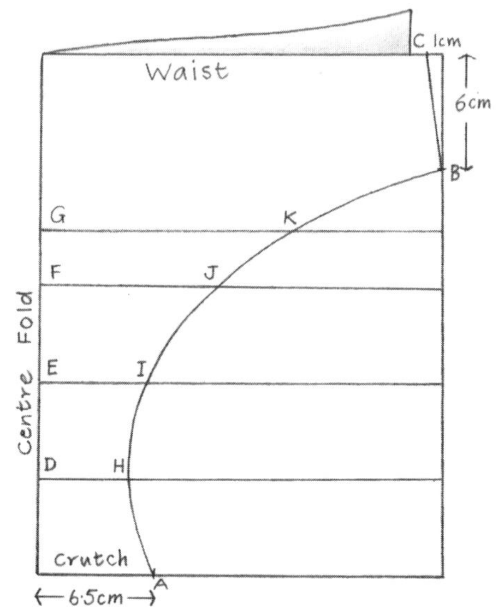

Cut this shape out, unfold it, and you have a piece like this:

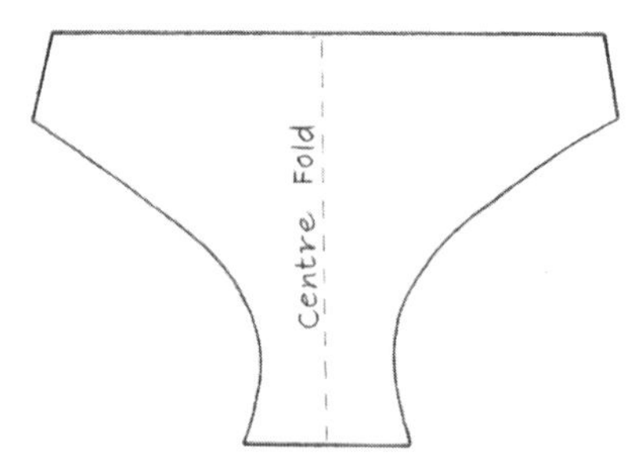

For the bra you only need to cut out one paper pattern piece. Having cut out one bust cup in fabric, just turn the pattern over for the other one.

On your paper rectangle measure 2cm in from the top right-hand corner. That's A. From the bottom right-hand corner measure up 2cm – B. Join A to B. Along the bottom edge measure in 5cm – C. Join BC. Cut out this modified rectangle paper pattern.

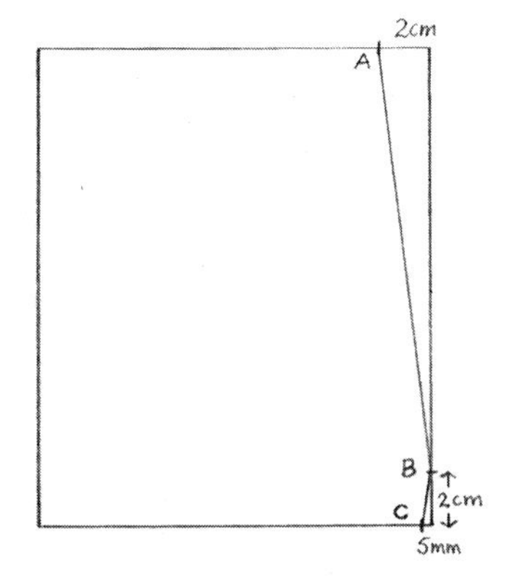

Cut out one piece of fabric and one piece of lining for each boob – four pieces all together.

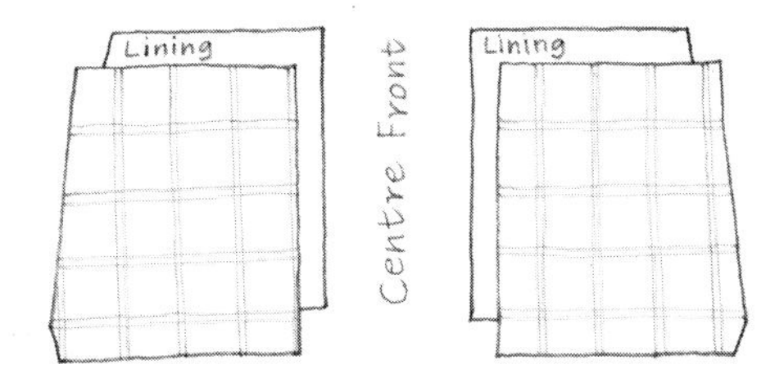

If there's a distinctive pattern printed on your fabric, cut the pieces out wisely. An enormous red rose on the left and a mere bud with a couple of leaves on the right could appear a trifle odd.

Making the bikini top

You make up each bust cup separately, but obviously the procedure's exactly the same for the left as for the right. Lay the right side of the fabric to the lining (so that the wrong side of the fabric is uppermost). Sewing 1cm in, sew the fabric to the lining down the centre-front edge and down the outer ABC edge. This makes a kind of tube. Turn the tube right side out and iron it flat. If the material you are using is nice and firm, zigzag, straight machine or hand oversew the fabric to the lining along the top and bottom edges (stitching close to the edge), not making any turning but just joining the two layers of material together. Single turn the top (the narrow end) over 1·5cm and sew it down as close to the edge as possible, over the previous stitching. Single turn the bottom edge 2cm and sew it too. (With materials which fray easily it would be more secure to make a double turning top and bottom – first a narrow turning, and then a wide one to form the channel for the laces.)

Now all you've got to do is to thread the laces through like this and your bikini top is complete.

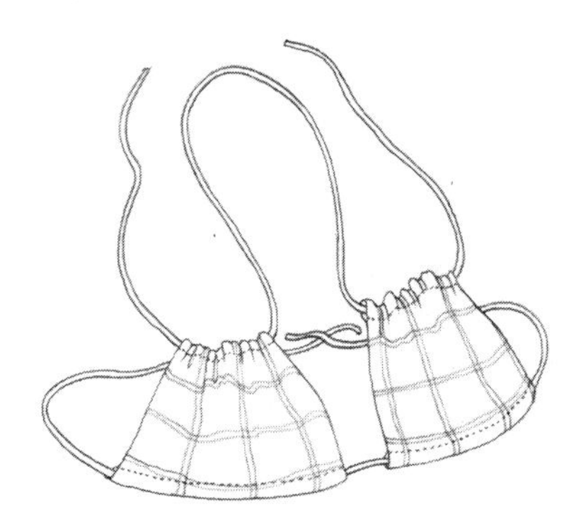

For a very small bust, decrease the height of the bust cup pieces, not the width.

Making the pants

Pin the paper pattern shapes to your fabric and cut out two front pieces; one in your fabric and one in the lining. Do the same for the back. Arrange them in a pile in this order with the crutch edges all lined up.

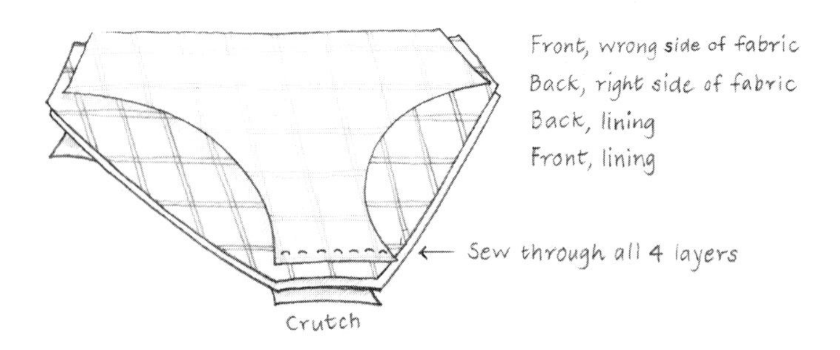

Sew the crutch seam 15mm in through all four fabrics. Open the pants out so that you have:

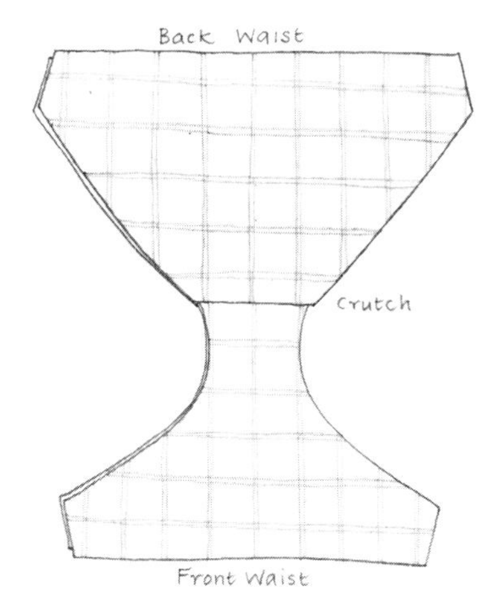

Now sew all the way round the edge of the shape to hold the two layers of fabric together. Zigzagging is best for this but straight machining or hand oversewing will do.

With the wrong side of the pants out, turn a single 1·5cm hem all round the leg part and sew it down (over the previous stitching). Thread the 40cm bits of elastic through each of the leg hems. Be sure to sew the elastic down securely at each end.

Sew a single turning 2cm deep on each waist edge. Thread and secure the 33cm length of elastic through the back, the 24cm length through the front.

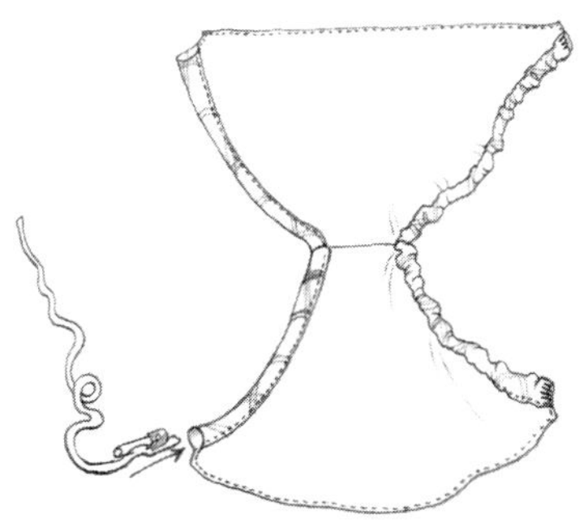

Turn each of the four corner points of the pants over once 2cm and double sew them down very firmly. Thread a lace through each corner and knot it. Wear your bikini pants with the front and back laces knotted on the hips.

Semicircular summer dress

This charming dress will fit anybody because the shoulder straps are adjustable, making the bodice the size required. The dress in the photograph is trimmed with another material – in the same colour and check pattern, but on a different scale. It has extras, i.e. the bottom edging, the pocket and the scarf. For the straps and edging you could use braid or bias ribbon as a contrast but you can make the entire basic garment out of two squares of fabric, each measuring 110 × 110cm.

The front and back are exactly the same. Using the string and chalk technique explained on page 69, draw an arc, radius 110cm on each piece of fabric. Again as on page 69, you make a paper pattern shape for the neck hole. Here the neck hole is an even horseshoe shape.

Put the point of your compasses in a right-angle corner of the piece of paper and draw a 10cm radius arc. Now, round the outside of this, draw another arc, radius 15cm. Fold the paper in half (as if preparing to make a paper dart). Freehand, draw, as nicely as you can, a curve from the 10cm arc at the outer edge of the paper to the 15cm arc on the fold. Cut this shape out through the double thickness. If the centre of your horseshoe is rather pointed when you open the paper out, trim it to a better rounded shape.

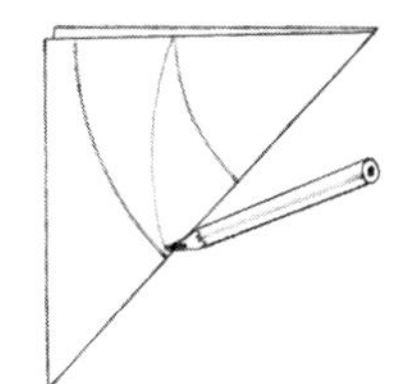

Pin this paper neck pattern in the corner of the fabric and cut out the back and front pieces of the dress.

The straps-cum-binding are made from two strips of material, each 125 × 4cm, cut on the cross (that is, diagonally; at an angle of 45° to the straight threads of which the material is made). You can get these out of your left-over fabric but they will have to be joined. The material is cut on the cross so that it will bend nicely round the curves. Bias binding (as this is called) is stretchy, so it gives. Straight binding would pucker up round curves.

You have two pieces of left-over fabric this shape:

Fold a piece in half like this:

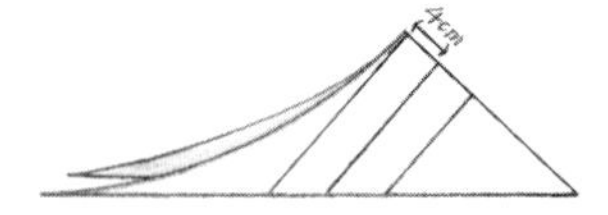

On the fold line, starting by the curve, measure along and mark two points, 4cm apart. Draw lines at right angles to the fold from these marks to the bottom edge. Cut along these lines, through the double thickness. Do this with the other left-over piece too. You'll then have four strips. As you need two 125cm lengths here is the joining method. Pin together two pieces, right sides together, at right angles:

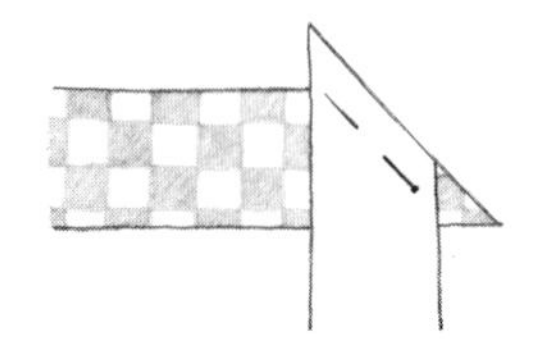

Open the binding out to be sure it's going to make a smooth continuous piece and is not going to join in a step. This settled, sew the little seam, press it open and snip off the excess triangle. Sew up the sides seams of the dress 1cm in to within 25cm of the top (the pointed end). Finish off the raw edges along the seams and right up to the top of the dress. (See page 20 for how to finish seams.)
Press the seams flat and also a single 1cm turning on each unsewn 25cm length. Sew round these 25cm slits, which are the armholes.

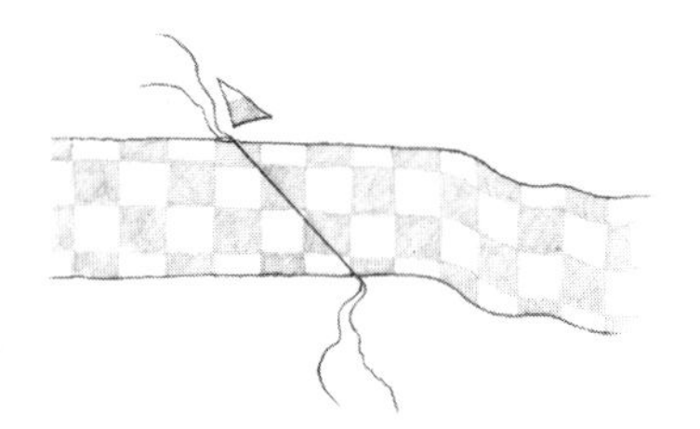

At the neck, both on the front and the back, pin three tiny evenly spaced tucks so that the neck curve, when you measure it by bending your tape measure round, is now 19cm long. Sew the tiny tucks down.

Cut the two bias binding strips down to 125cm. Press little single turnings under at the extreme ends of each. Fold each strip in half to find the centre and chalk-mark it. Find and mark the centre of the neck hole, front and back, in the same way. Put the right side of the centre of the strap/binding to the right side of the centre of the neck and pin the strap/binding around the neck curve. Stitch it 1cm in from the edge.

Fold the strap/binding over to the wrong side of the neck hole. Turn it under once 1cm and pin it down round the neck curve. Now, folding both sides of the binding under once 1cm, pin it all the way along the entire strap. Sewing close to the lower edge, stitch all along the strap and through the neck curve.

Double turn and sew a 1cm hem round the bottom of the dress – the basic shape is completed.

The pocket

To make a heart-shaped pocket cut out two heart shapes that are 1cm bigger all round than the required pocket. Pin the two pieces, right sides together, and sew them 1cm in all the way round except for 5cm left open on one of the straight sides. Cut little nicks out of the curved parts, across the bottom and between the two cheeks. This helps the shape turn right side out neatly – which you now do, with the aid of a pin for the pointed end. Iron it flat, turning the unsewn section in to line up. Try the dress on to find out the best position for the pocket. Pin it in position and attach it by sewing near the edge round the lower portion of it. This takes care of the little unsewn section, by the way. It sounds daft, but do remember it is a pocket. Don't find yourself happily sewing all the way round. That way it becomes a patch!

Apply this approach to pockets of any shape you like.

Conversions

Shirt tales

Men's shirts are frequently discarded by their owners (or maybe their owner's wives) when there's plenty of life left in them. Standards at the office must be very high because cast-off shirts are often in really good condition.

This versatile garment can obviously be worn simply as a shirt or an overshirt but from the point of view of a girl there are likely to be three drawbacks. These are: (1) the shoulders are absurdly wide; (2) the sleeves are too long and (3) the collar and cuffs are a bit frayed. The following ideas get round these three problems and give you quite a few style variations. They are all simple to carry out; after all, the hard work has already been done in the actual making of the shirt.

The manly shoulders problem

Tucked yoke

This first method works best on thin fabric – which is what the majority of shirts are made of. Pin tiny tucks across on the shoulder, extending down the front of the shirt to just above your bust and down the back some 28cm or so from the middle of the shoulders. Pin as many tucks as you need to take up the length of each shoulder. The outer tucks may tail off and be shorter than those in the centre. Sew the tucks down, using backstitching at either end. This is a neat solution that gives the shirt an attractive smock-like fullness.

Strong-coloured stitching looks very good on a white or pale-coloured shirt. You could echo this by adding lines of stitching in the same colour on the cuffs and collar.

Peasant style

Another variation is useful if the shoulders need only a little shortening and also if the fabric is a bit thicker. You'll require some decorative ribbon or tape. The style shown in the photograph takes about 5 metres of tape, 3cm wide. Of course you can invent your own designs by attaching the ribbon in different ways. There are certain lightweight types of webbing, plain or with a coloured pattern woven in, which are very cheap to buy. Or you could print some plain coloured tape with your own personal pattern all the way along it. (See page 173.)

Take just one tuck on each side to reduce the shoulders to the correct size. As in the previous example the tucks go from just above the bust, over the shoulder and down the back to the shoulder blade. Sew the two tucks down. Cut two pieces of tape 15mm longer than the tucks and sew them over the tucks. Do this by sewing all the way round close to the edge of the tape and making little turnings at the ends. Now add horizontal pieces running across the shirt from the ends of the first tapes, back and front. Run a tape down each side of the centre fastening. Sew tapes from under the collar along the shoulders and right down the outside of the sleeves, finishing with a band just above the cuffs. As well as concealing the alteration this treatment makes a dull, ordinary white shirt into a cheerful peasant-style top.

Shirt jacket

This way of narrowing the shoulders, and at the same time making a really original shirt, suits a heavyish material like denim or thick tartan. It gives a sporty, outdoor look, ideal for wearing over a sweater, as the shirt practically becomes a jacket. You will need some extra fabric. If the shirt is very long you might be able to cut the bottom off and use it.

But you may prefer a contrasting material. Quilted fabric is ideal. Perhaps you can use part of a discarded quilted dressing-gown or buy a remnant of ready-quilted material. (How to make your own quilting: page 132.) Lightweight suede, suedette, chamois leather or PVC would be great, or you could use tweed or corduroy.

First take a tuck across the yoke of the shirt to make the shoulders the right size (details in the previous section). Put the shirt on and decide how far down, both at the back and the front, you want the new yoke to come. It can just imitate the original yoke or it can be extended into a more elaborate shape. Roughly mark with tailor's chalk the kind of shape you have in mind. Maybe a friend could draw on the back for you.

Have ready a pencil and some tracing paper (greaseproof is OK). Lay the shirt down with one shoulder opened out and facing you. On the shirt mark the centre of the back below the collar and lay the tracing paper on top. You only need to draw half the shape. The other half is a mirror image so all you need to do is turn the tracing paper over. Trace the two curves where the collar and the sleeve join on to the shirt. From your tailor's chalk marks draw out your design for the yoke. This drawing can now be cut out and used as a pattern to cut round. (Don't forget it's only half the shape.)

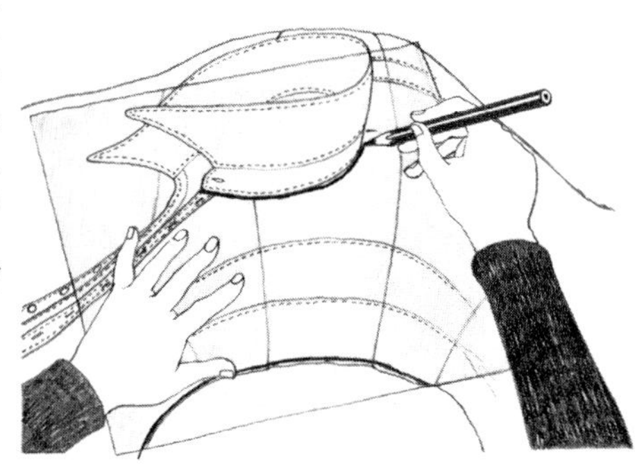

If you are going to sew on a non-fraying material like suede or PVC you don't have to allow for turnings. Should you want fringing you must of course allow enough material for that. It's easiest to sew the piece on first and cut the fringe afterwards – just straight cuts up to within 5mm of the sewn line.

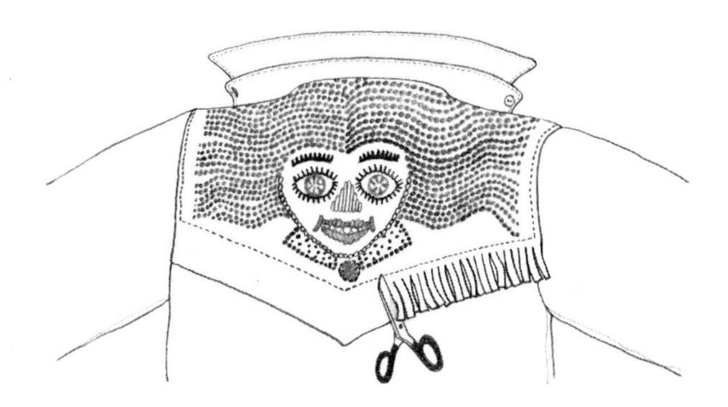

For fabrics that do fray and will need to be turned under once allow 1cm all the way round. Cut little nicks out round the curves to help the curved sections turn under neatly.

If you intend to embroider the yoke do it now, before you sew it on to the shirt.

With quilted fabrics cut the shape out with the turning allowance and turn it under like other fabrics. Pin and then sew the yoke piece on to the shirt. Matching elbow patches are fun too. They have to be sewn on by hand unless your machine has a special sleeve device. A belt in the same material as the yoke would be rather good too – either a tie belt or one with a buckle.

When he sees yours your boyfriend will want his shirt tarted up too!

What to do about sleeves that are too long

Apart from merely rolling them up, the easiest way to deal with sleeves that flap over the hands is to turn the cuffs back. Remove the buttons and sew them on again on the other side of the cuff, which was formerly the inside. If necessary move the buttons along a bit too to make the cuff tighter.

Another answer is to take one or two tucks to reduce the length of the sleeves. Covered by decorative tape they'd make a nice addition to the peasant style already mentioned. Experiment first by wrapping the tape around the sleeve while you are wearing the shirt. This helps you to find the best looking positions for the tucks.

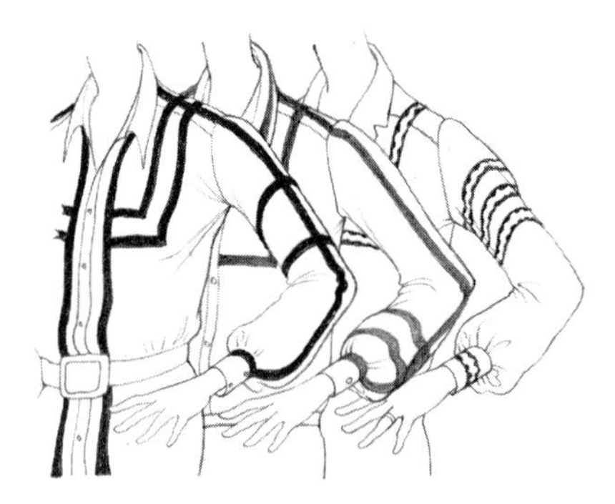

A feminine look is achieved with gathered bands around the sleeves. Take a tuck and sew it down along either edge to form a channel. Leave a tiny bit unsewn so that you can thread some elastic through. Knot it at the right length to gather the sleeve in sufficiently. Sew up the little open gap. Once again you can experiment to find the best place to put the tuck (or tucks).

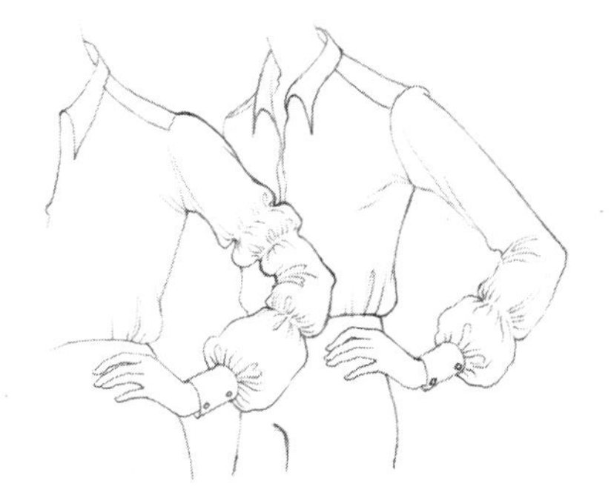

Or adapt this very ancient form of sleeve decoration:

Maybe the Romans didn't use this device just to shorten their sleeves, but there is no reason why you shouldn't. Join two ribbons to the shirt below the shoulder on the arm-hole seam, one at the front and one at the back. You'll have to ask some-one to criss-cross and tie them for you (unless you happen to be a contortionist). Add another ribbon wrapped around under the bust. For parties wouldn't tinsel be dazzling?

Good-bye scruffy cuffs and threadbare collar

Just cut them off! Try some of these conversions.

Scoop neck

For this one you'll need some narrow elastic. Elasticated styles are only suitable for lightweight fabrics. First put the shirt on and with tailor's chalk roughly mark the sort of scoop neck you want and also the sleeve length. Take the shirt off and lay it flat on the table with the front facing you. Fasten the buttons. Neaten up the roughly drawn curve, which is part of a circle. To do this find the centre point of the circle. It's generally around the area of the label in the back of the neck. You can use a pin to mark the spot, or tailor's chalk. Holding the end of your tape measure or ruler on this centre point measure out the radius of the circle *minus* 2cm for the turning. Mark the distance several times so that you can build up a complete curve. The curve you have drawn is smaller than the final scoop will be because of the turning allowance. Make the curve come about 3cm above a button.

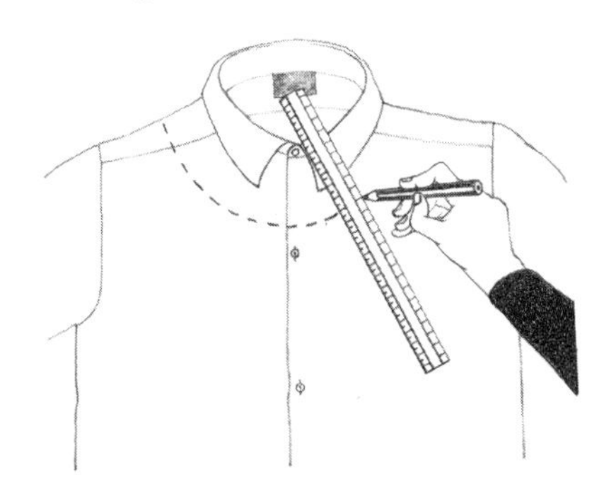

Be sure the shirt is laid out completely flat, back and front – no crinkles. Now cut the scoop shape out, cutting through both the front and the back of the shirt.

Add on the 2cm for turnings to the sleeve length you require. Cut the sleeves off straight across.

Double turn the rough edges of the neck and sleeves, pin and sew them. Thread elastic through each hem and fasten it securely at all the ends. Part of the slit of the original sleeve opening may still remain. If so, thread your elastic right round inside the new sleeve hem and fasten it. Sew up the wrist end of the gap and finish it off by adding a button from one of the cuffs you have cut off. If the neck fastening gapes a bit add a concealed hook and eye to hold it down.

This style can be worn with a belt or loose. Or you can gather the waist with a row or two of shirring (page 44). Work the shirring from just in front of the side seams either all the way across the back or just in short sections at the sides. Either of these looks better than gathering up the whole waist – and it avoids any messing about with the front fastenings.

Gipsy blouse

This design – very cool and summery – is a variation on the previous one. Alter the neck in just the same way. Decide on the sleeve length. This can be short as illustrated or three-quarter length. With the latter you have a choice of wearing your sleeves at three-quarter length or pushing them up to appear shorter. Allow an additional 6cm of fabric on the length of the sleeve for the gathering and the hem. Cut the sleeves off. Double turn and sew a narrow hem. To gather up the sleeve you can use the shirring technique (page 44). Work one row of shirring 2cm in from the hemmed edge. Leave a space of 1cm and then work the second row. An alternative to shirring is to sew a narrow tuck 2cm in from the edge and thread elastic through it.

Cut the body of the shirt off just below waist level. Hem the bottom. Leave 2cm of fabric and then sew four rows of shirring spaced 1cm apart. Another way of gathering the waist is to sew on elastic webbing. You can buy it in a haberdashery store. There is a delicious chenille version available in lovely colours.

Blouson

Here is a shirt converted into a blouson (that's French for a kind of floppy overshirt). Make the elasticated scoop neck as explained above. Cut the shirt off straight across just below your hipline. If it's a shirt that has tails, cut just above the side vents. Cut the sleeves off, hem the cut edges and thread them with elastic as explained for the elasticated yoke and cuffs style on page 95. Omit the button.

Turn the bottom hem up first 1cm and then 2cm and sew it. This makes a channel for the drawstring. If the shirt has a short front fastening you will have to cut two vertical 15mm slits through the front thickness of the hem that you've just sewn, with 5cm space between the two slits. These are to thread the drawstring through. Blanket stitch round the slits. Thread some attractive ribbon or cord through the channel. (An economy hint is to use cheap tape for the part of the drawstring that doesn't show round the back.) Tie some bows of ribbon or cord and sew them on to the sleeves to masquerade as drawstrings. Trying to tie bows on your own arms just isn't worth the effort! Why not add some bobbles and/or something silly like lots of little plastic pigs. You can buy pendant-type little pigs and things – or even cheaper – a bag of toy farmyard animals.

Ribbed neck and cuffs version

This garment is a cross between a shirt and a sweater. It's a good way of using up a sweater that is now either too short for you in the body and arms or has gone all baggy at the back. (See the photo on page 98.)

Cut the scoop neck out of the shirt by the method already explained. Do the same thing with the sweater. Cut the shirt sleeves off above the cuff opening slit. Cut suitable sleeve lengths from the sweater. Turn the knitted collar piece inside out. Pin its right side to the right side of the shirt all the way round the scoop neck. Then sew the two together being careful not to stretch the knitting.

For a shorter top cut the shirt off at the waist. Finish it off by sewing on a band of ribbing from the sweater. If the ribbing is a bit past it (all baggy) use elastic webbing instead. The same applies to the sleeves too.

How to convert a shirt into a dress

For each of these schemes you'll need some additional material. You can make use of things like remnants, dresses and skirts you've grown out of or bits of sheet or curtains. The weight of the fabric should be the same as that of the shirt. Choose patterns and colours that combine in an interesting way. For instance, if the shirt is striped, try a combination of different types of stripes and checks. If you need to do so apply any of the methods already explained to deal with the three bugbears of too-wide shoulders, too-long sleeves and tatty cuffs and collar.

LE
FRANÇAIS
ACTUEL

Shirt dress

This style, which can be any length you choose, is really just an elongated shirt, to be worn loose or belted.

The sleeves, the collar and a yoke-shaped piece of the top of the shirt are retained, together with part of the front fastening section. The rest of the dress is made up from horizontal bands of different fabrics in various widths. The lower part of the shirt that was cut off is used here to make some of the bands.

This is how you cut the shirt down to start with. Put the shirt on and mark the point, just above the waist, where the front fastening will end. Make it come in between two of the buttons. Now lay the shirt out flat on the table, front uppermost. On the front side which has the buttons line up the end of your ruler with the outside edge of the shirt front. Fasten the buttons, still holding the ruler in place. The buttonhole side of the shirt front will partially cover the ruler. From the edge of the buttonhole side, on the bit of ruler that's sticking out, measure along 15mm and mark it on the button-bearing side. This is length A.

Now mark this same measurement A on the buttonhole side of the shirt front, measuring from the edge across. Mark the measurement twice on the lower part of the front fastening on each side and draw lines to link the marks together.

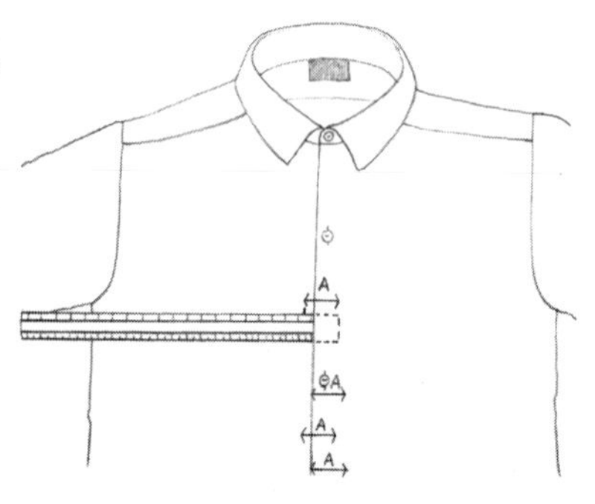

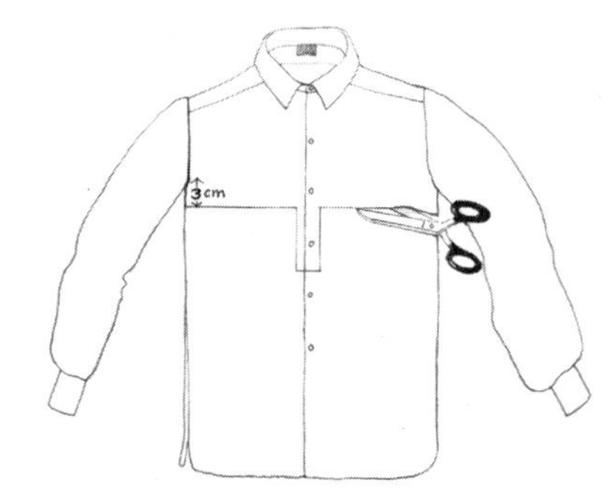

From each underarm (where the sleeve is set into the shirt) measure 3cm down. Draw a straight line across the shirt at this point. Now cut the shirt top off by cutting along this line and round the front fastening line. Except when you are cutting out the front fastening cut through the front and back of the shirt together.

Make the first band of different fabric extend from the bottom of the yoke piece down to the bottom of the front fastening. Measure this distance and add on 15mm for the turning that will occur when you join this band to the yoke part of the shirt. Now measure the distance round the shirt at this point. Do this by measuring the corresponding part of the piece of the shirt you've just cut off. Add on 3cm for turnings. Fasten the buttons and also pin the fastening together to stop it flapping about. With right sides together pin the ends of the new band to the edges of the fastening section. Pin with a view to making a 15cm deep seam. Line up the bottom edge of the fastening section with the bottom edge of the band. Sew the band to the fastening section. Now pin and sew the top edge of the band to the yoke piece.

Plan the rest of the dress by trying the top on and holding the different fabrics round yourself. Decide how deep you want each band to be and the order in which they are to be arranged.

Cut all the bands out to give you the front and back pieces. There will be side seams. Allow 2cm for turnings on each side of each piece. On a short dress the skirt part of the dress can be the same width as the shirt top, so it's straight all the way down. On a long dress, even though there are slits, you must make the skirt gradually slope out so that you can be sure of walking comfortably. The easiest way to assemble the front and back pieces into this sloping shape is to cut each band slightly wider as you get towards the bottom. Sew them all together along the horizontal joins. Then lay the complete front and back pieces out flat. On the hipline of each piece measure out and draw a line the same length as the distance across the shirt back. From each end of this line draw a line at a right angle down to the bottom of the skirt. On each side mark 5cm outside the line. Now draw lines from these 5cm points up to the ends of the hipline to give the correct slope to cut along.

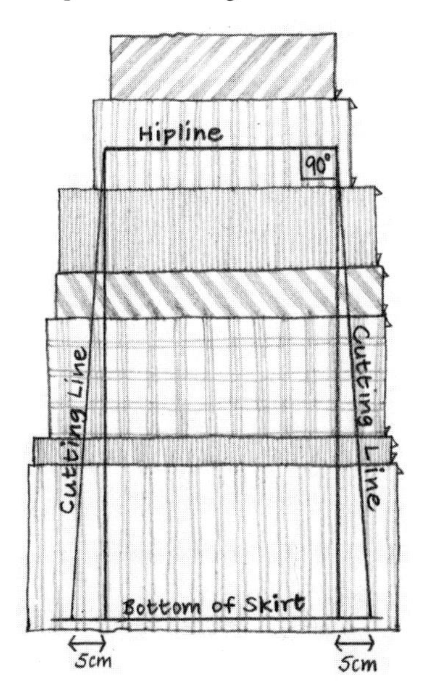

Having cut the front and back pieces out sew the side seams 2cm in down as far as the slits. Sew the skirt to the bodice. Double turn and hem the slits at the sides and the bottom hem.

A rather classy touch is to bind the hem and side slits with a broad bias binding cut from the original shirt material. If you intend to do this cut curves on the bottom corners of the slits as it's easier to work the binding round a curve than a right angle – it looks good too. (How to cut out and apply bias binding is explained on page 84.)

Dress with gathered skirt

Here's a dress that uses the top bit of a shirt (the bit that's difficult to make) as a high bodice with a full gathered skirt. Cut the top part of the shirt off along a straight line 3cm below the bottom of your bust. Cut straight through the front fastening.

Make the skirt from two rectangles of fabric each 91cm wide × whatever length of skirt you choose.

Sew the bottom of the shirt fastening together. Run a line of shirring 3cm from the edge to gather up the bottom of the shirt. It should fit snugly under the bust. (Shirring directions are on page 44.)

Sew the two side seams of the skirt. Sew a line of shirring 3cm from the top edge. Gather the skirt up so that it fits on to the bottom edge of the bodice. Join the skirt and the bodice with a seam 1·5cm in.

The pretty frill along the bottom of the skirt is made by joining together pieces of the cut-off part of the shirt with other suitable fabrics. Make the frill as deep as you fancy. It has to be 367cm long to gather up and go right round the bottom of the dress. (The instructions on how to make and sew on a frill like this are given on page 46.)

Finish your dress off by adding some contrasting ribbon around the bodice join and, if you like, round the skirt above the frill.

This is an excellent style for a fatty.

Dress with a tiered skirt

The pretty, flouncy style shown here starts with a shirt converted as on page 95, using shirring at the waist, neck and cuffs. You then add as many flounces (frills) as you want to.

Cut the shirt off straight across the hip-line. Work out how long the first frill should be by measuring round the bottom edge of the shirt. Double this measurement and that's the length of the frill. The depth is up to you. As you go down the skirt each successive frill is twice as long as the one above it. Each frill is gathered along the top with two lines of stitching. All the details on joining frills on are to be found on page 46.

With scraps of the different fabrics used for the frills make a little pocket and hanky and plait a multi-coloured tie belt (page 26).

Crazy patchwork dress

Here's a nice loony idea. Extend a shirt like this. Take it to any length (or lengths) you like by adding on a wild mixture of crazy patchwork and ridiculous bits and pieces. (The crazy patchwork technique is explained on page 120.)

Looks a bit dull?

You've altered your shirt to fit well. You've completed the conversion from shirt to dress. Although the new garments are fine and functional perhaps they are lacking that unique, personal look? Turn to the decoration chapter for some ideas to make them really special.

Certain types of decoration lend themselves to shirt-based clothing. The embroidery in lines that you can do on the most elementary of sewing machines is just right to go with machined tucks on the shoulders. Go mad with zigzags and wiggly lines. A great idea would be to base your design on an Olde English smock pattern – the type worn by straw-chewing yokels. You could work it in beige on a cream or beige shirt. Or try printing a simple little motif over and over again all round the edges of the collar of a shirt, down either side of the front fastening, round the cuffs and wherever else you feel inclined. (See page 174.)

Pyjama jacket

A man's pyjama jacket may not look very promising but with very little effort you can convert it into an attractive casual jacket.

If the material looks too pyjama-ish consider dyeing it. If it's striped you can achieve some very subtle striping; if plain try batik or tie and dye (see pages 146–57). A pyjama cord dyes well too.

The waist and cuffs of the finished jacket have drawstrings. Pyjama jackets have often lost most of their buttons but, in any case, they are very dull! Add some more interesting ones or make Chinese ball buttons from cord to match the drawstrings. (See how to make these on page 27.)

You will need a length of inexpensive tape 3cm wide and long enough to go round the waist of the jacket (not gathered up). And you'll require some attractive ribbon or cord, long enough to go round your waist and tie in a bow and also to go round each wrist and tie. This could be dyed pyjama cord. If you're making Chinese ball buttons you will need 25cm of cord per button. To economize you can make those parts of the drawstrings that are permanently concealed out of something really cheap like tape. Just attach short lengths of exotic ribbon or cord at the business ends. For further thoughts on cords have a look at plaiting and braiding on page 25.

Try the jacket on and fasten the buttons. If at this stage they are missing, pin the fronts together where the buttons should be. Decide at what level you want the waist to be. At this waist level measure out 8cm from the centre of the front to each side. Mark these two points with pins.

On the inside of the jacket rule a line at waist level from pin to pin right round across the two fronts and the back. With this line running through the centre, pin on the inexpensive tape. Then sew it to the jacket by running two lines of stitching as close as you can safely get to the outer edge of the tape. Make little turnings to finish it off at either end. Where the ends of the tape come cut two 15mm vertical slits in the fabric of the jacket. Blanket stitch round these.

Unless you are very tall or have arms like an orang-utang the sleeves of the jacket are likely to be too long for you. If they are, take a tuck on the inside, which will become the channel for the drawstring. With the jacket inside out, measure 8cm from the cuff edge up the sleeve and mark that distance. Put the jacket on, still inside out, and pin a tuck in each sleeve 8cm from the cuff, that reduces it to the right length for you. Sew this and then, laying the tuck flat against the sleeve sew another line of stitching 3cm up through it. Turn the jacket right side out. On the outside of the wrist, in line with the tuck, make two vertical slits 15mm long through just the outer layer of fabric. These should be 8cm apart. Blanket stitch round these four holes. (If you are an orang-utang make the sleeve drawstring channels in the same way as at the waist – with tape.)

Thread the appropriate length of cord through each of the three drawstring channels with the ends coming through the holes for tying purposes. Stitch through the centre back of the waist channel and the cord (just a few stitches) to stop the cord escaping. (This is a good tip for pyjamas in their natural state.) Do the same thing with the sleeve ties by catching them with a stitch or two on the inside of the sleeve. Either keep the wrist ties permanently tied, allowing just enough room to get your hands through, or make sure there's someone around to tie them for you (very tricky alone).

You too can be a jeanius

Everybody becomes passionately fond of their jeans and it's a sad day when you realize they really are getting a bit past it. The following pages suggest some ways in which you can recycle jeans and trousers.

A useful tip about sewing thick denim is to make sure your needle is really sharp – a nice, new, thick one. Otherwise, machining will be heavy going and hand sewing sheer agony.

Use the same colour thread as the jeans manufacturer has used. Copy the style of stitching too – two lines of stitching if that's what has been used elsewhere. If your lines of machine stitching look rather weedy compared with those on the jeans try using double thread. If your machine has two spool pins (the spikes where you put the cotton reels) and you've got two reels of the same colour, fine. Just thread the machine up with the two threads in the usual way, putting them both through the eye of the needle. If your machine has only one spool pin, wind the thread on two bobbins and place them, one on top of the other, on the single spool pin. Then thread up as before.

For hand sewing use backstitch with a double thread for strength.

Short stories

Cutting down an old pair of jeans to convert them into shorts is nothing new but here are a few further ideas on the subject.

They can be short shorts. If they are going to be very brief, put the jeans on and then get a friend to chalk a line round both your legs where you want the finished line of the shorts to be. If you were to simply cut them straight across they would do this:

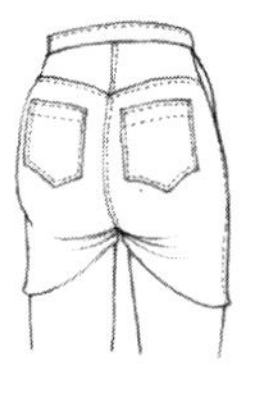

So to make them fit properly they must follow the contours of your thighs.

Remove the jeans. Lay them flat on the table and mark a line all the way round 2·5cm below the line your friend has already drawn. Cut the legs off round this line. Turn a double hem up to the original line and sew it.

Conversions

Try Bermuda shorts or somewhere in between them and short shorts. For the longer types of shorts you can cut the legs of your jeans off straight across. But do try them on first and chalk mark the finished length. Why not start with Bermudas? If you look ridiculous, cut them shorter. Bermudas tend to look best on girls with long slim legs.

The bottom edges can be cut into a fringe and encouraged to fray. Or they can be bound with fabric or braid in a contrasting colour – bound slits at the sides would be amusing; and then you might use the same binding or braid elsewhere – round the pockets, as a tie belt or as some crazy braces.

Why not decorate your shorts absolutely all over? See the decoration chapters for inspiration.

Knickerbocker glories

If you have a pair of fairly baggy trousers that are too short for you, cut them off some 15cm below the knee and make nice turn-ups (iron-on hemming web might be useful here). You'll have a pair of very smart gauchos, really stylish worn with high boots, thick, patterned tights or over-the-knee socks.

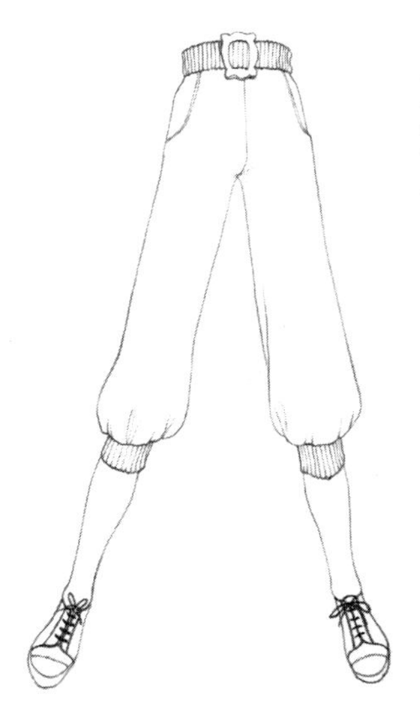

Another remedy for too-short jeans or trousers is to cut them off, again below the knee, and sew on elasticated webbing – very sporty. What about a belt of the same webbing too? Just add a suitable buckle from your hoard.

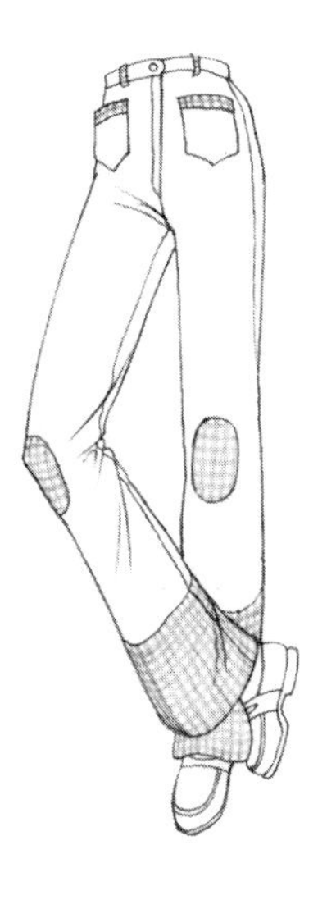

A tall story

To lengthen a pair of jeans so that it appears intentional, choose, for your additions, a material that looks interesting alongside the jeans fabric – but that's also washable.

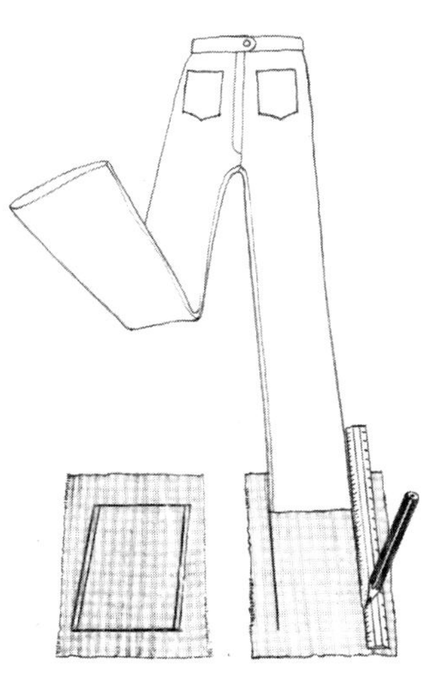

You will need to cut out four pieces of the additional fabric, two for each leg. Do it two at a time. Lay the trouser bottoms flat on the double layers of cloth. Use your ruler, lined up against each side seam of the trousers, to extend the line on each side as far as you want the extra bit to go. Add on 4cm for turnings. Now mark a point 1cm up from the bottom edge of the trousers on either side of the leg.

Lift the jeans away from the fabric. Draw a line joining up those two 1cm points. Draw lines parallel to, but 1cm outside, the extended leg lines. (All these 1cm away lines are for the seam allowances.) Complete the shape by drawing the line across the bottom.

Cut these four pieces out. Make two tubes (which may slope out a bit) by sewing them up at the sides, wrong sides together, allowing a 1cm seam.

With the tube inside out pin and sew it to the trouser bottom 1cm in, like this:

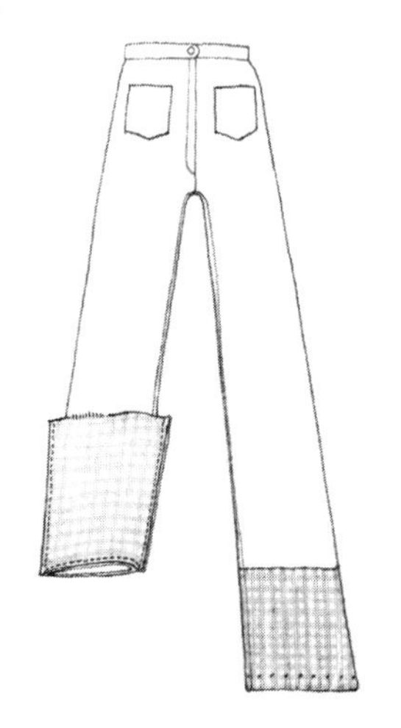

Turn it down, right side out, and make a 3cm deep double hem along the bottom. Add some of this material elsewhere – perhaps two patch pockets on your backside; or replace all the belt loops with it.

Morning glory

For early morning jogging round the park (or early morning lolling on the bed) make yourself a simple but snug track suit. Make the top as shown on page 64 and the bottom by converting a pair of suitably thinnish, stretchy trousers. Cut off the trouser bottoms so that they are 20cm from your ankle bone. Sew on two suitable lengths of cut-off (or specially knitted) jumper sleeves. These are sewn on in the same way as the top.

Jeans into a short skirt

Sometimes you just feel like wearing a skirt but you don't want to give up the casual jeans feeling – so make yourself a jeans skirt.

If you are one of those girls who just doesn't seem to get any fatter, just higher and higher, and your jean bottoms are at mid-calf – this is for you.

First unpick the whole of each inside leg seam. At the front of the jeans unpick the seam which runs up from the crutch to the bottom of the fly. Then lay the jeans out flat on the table, back uppermost, and start unpicking the centre-back seam from the crutch upwards. Unpick until the garment will lie flat when one side of the back crutch seam is laid over the other. It should now start to resemble a skirt shape. Still at the back, pin the top overlapping piece to the equivalent lower piece. Turn the garment over and pin the front overlapping sections in the same way. At the front you won't get such a big overlap as at the back. Jeans are shaped at the back to go under your bottom.

Ask a friend to measure you from your waist to your knee. With the jeans still laid out flat, front side up, mark that length, plus 3cm for the hem, from the waist down the centre of each leg. Rule a straight line through these two marks. Cut the lower part of the legs off through this line. That will give you two spare rectangles of fabric to use to fill in the empty triangular spaces at the centre front and the centre back of your skirt. Making sure the garment is lying out flat and looking skirt-shaped, slide one of the spare cut-off pieces under the front triangular space, spreading it out underneath what were formerly the jean legs. These leg pieces should still have their edges turned under. Pin the piece of fabric in place. Do likewise with the triangular area at the back. Sew each triangle into place using the same colour thread as was originally used to make the jeans. Trim off the excess fabric.

Turn the bottom edge of your skirt up with a double turning and sew it. Alternatively cut and fray out a rough fringe along the hemline.

Jeans into a long skirt

To make a long jeans skirt you will need some additional fabric to fill in the long triangles at the front and back because here you keep the trouser legs at their original length.

Follow the first steps of how to make a short jeans skirt up to the point where you cut the legs off. Obviously you don't do that.

You can be really inventive about the way in which you fill in the two triangles. The previous section tells you how to cut and sew them on.

Too tall?

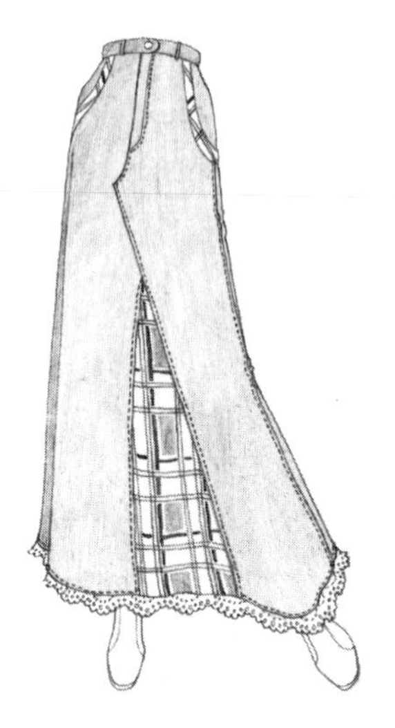

If the skirt is too short because you have grown out of the jeans add some clever additions at the hem.

Here are some ideas:

Fill in the triangles with tartan and add a lacy mock-petticoat along the bottom. Sew the lace (perhaps from an old curtain or the edging of a tablecloth) inside the skirt so that it looks like a real petticoat peeping out.

Use a denim patchwork (see page 120) to complete the skirt, perhaps sewn with different brightly coloured threads. You can cut fringes and/or fray all the bottom pieces and other bits here and there.

Or use a mixed patchwork made from fabrics of a similar weight to the denim or whatever cloth your jeans are made from.

Fill in the triangular spaces with a patterned material and add appliquéd shapes (see page 170) to the denim. This is an excellent solution to worn knees or torn backsides!

Another way to lengthen the skirt is to cut some long strips of fabric, gather them on one side, hem the other side and sew them on as tiers. Fancy trimmings (maybe braid from some old curtains) would be fun along all seams. One tier on its own makes a good frill along the bottom. (How to add a fancy frill is explained on page 46.)

Too fat?

Maybe your jeans are now too small round the waist and hips? You can still make them into a long skirt. Follow the previous instructions and insert a fabric triangle in the front. However, at the back, unpick the entire back seam from the crutch to the waistband. If there is a belt loop at the centre back remove it. Cut through the centre of the waistband. Lay the garment, back uppermost, and part the back seam until the waist and hip measurements, including the gap in the middle, correspond with your own measurements. If you want to, trim off some of the curved corner of the inside legs – the part that went under your bottom. Turn any raw edges under 1·5cm once and pin them.

Now, as with the triangle at the front, insert a new long section of fabric which tapers towards the waistband. Pin it into position allowing 2cm to stick up into the gap in the waistband and sew it with a double line of stitching.

To complete the waistband cut a rectangle of fabric (possibly denim to link up with the original waistband) which is 5cm longer than the gap and 2·5cm wider than the depth of the original waistband multiplied by 2. Turn the outside ends of this bit under about 2cm and pin them with the pins on the outside. Turn the skirt inside out. Pin the right side of the new piece to the wrong side of the skirt below the gap like this:

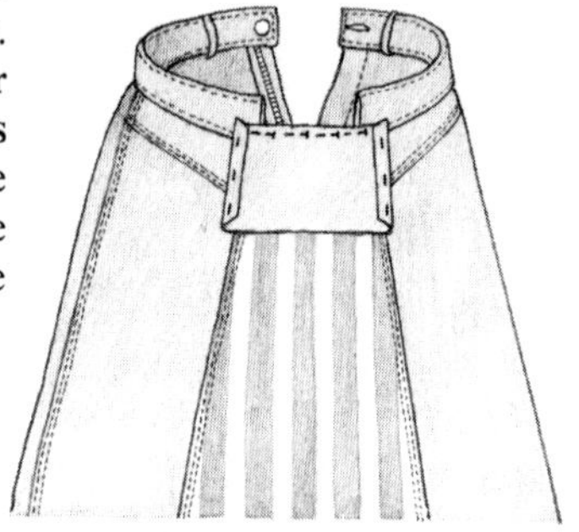

Sew along the pin line. Remove those pins.

Turn the skirt right side out again. Pull the denim piece over to the outside. Make a turning so that its lower edge will line up with the lower edge of the original waistband and pin it. Sew that short length and sew the two end sections securely to the original waistband. Remove all the pins. Replace the belt loop if you like, or, more craftily, cover the two new joins with two belt loops. Finish off the skirt by adding any decoration you fancy.

There's no end to the ideas once you get going. One of the good things about this type of garment is that you can add new bits at any time, whenever you feel like it or when there's a craze for something.

How to make skirts longer without anyone suspecting

So often dresses and skirts fit perfectly on the waist, bodice and hips but they are absurdly short. Try out these unusual remedies.

Frills and flounces

If it's a gathered skirt add a flounce or two in a fabric that teams well with the original. For instance, the addition of flowers on a different scale and in a different colour, but in the same weight of cloth, would look superb – and intentional.

Page 43 shows you how to calculate the size of a flounce (or frill) and page 46 shows how to sew it on. To make the whole thing totally convincing, cut a strip of the original skirt off the bottom and use this as a narrow binding over the stitching where you've joined on the new flounce(s).

On a dress you can add your own little touches, introducing some of the additional fabric into the bodice area. Be subtle though. Don't overdo it. A discreet edging to a pocket or a collar; belt loops or a covered buckle or buttons – that's the sort of thing. A triangular scarf worn on the head or round the shoulders is a winner too.

Decorative disguises

Sew a piece of contrasting coloured material to the skirt to make it the correct length. Hem the bottom. Now deliberately make use of the join by employing one or any combination of the techniques explained in the decoration chapter. This could be printing, bold embroidery – whatever you like. Use the motif(s) either side of the join and play around with the colours and the lights and darks.

Plus patchwork

Here you'll need patches in fabrics of a similar weight to the garment being lengthened.

Cut a band off the bottom of the skirt so that you've enough to make some patches in the original fabric too. Then extend the skirt by gradually adding whichever type of patchwork you prefer. (See the patchwork section, page 120.)

Cheating by dyeing

Before using any dyeing technique check that the original garment and the fabric with which you intend to lengthen it both accept the dye in the same way. Read through the dyeing chapter first.

Sew on your extra bit and hem it. Using a suitable method, such as fold and dip or batik, pattern dye either just the lower part of the skirt or the entire garment. Arrange it so that the join definitely gets dyed.

On a dress fold and dip would be very elegant at the hem and around the cuffs.

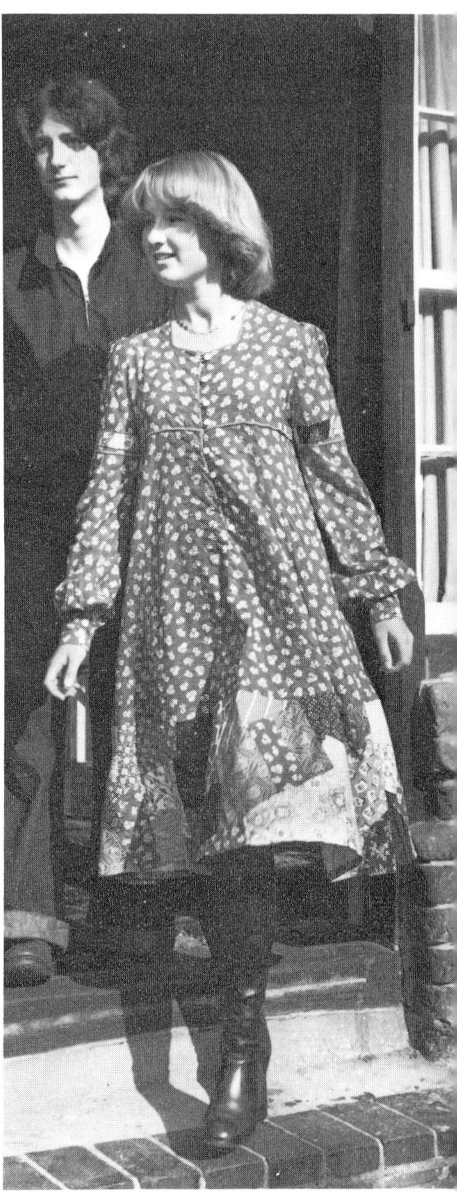

Making up your own fabrics

Patchwork

There are lots of books available on patchwork. Your library is bound to have at least one. Doing patchwork can be a most intricate and absorbing hobby. Here, however, just the very simplest methods and some new ideas are explained to enable you to use them in projects in this book. If you are a keen patchworker you can always substitute a more advanced form for that suggested in this book.

You can use any type of material for patchwork but don't mix the different types in the same garment. Keep to, for example, all cotton pieces for a skirt; all heavy tweed pieces for a waistcoat. Don't mix cotton and tweed.

Patchworking knitted material (cut from old sweaters) needs slightly different treatment and this is explained on page 128.

You can make up pieces of fabric by patchworking scraps together. Then these pieces of fabric can be used for lots of the ideas in this book. Each project shows you the shapes you need. On newspaper measure out and draw the shapes required for the garment you are making. You can then design your patchwork to fit into the shapes. This means you can distribute the colours around sensibly and, with any luck, you won't end up with a great glare of red on the bust and nowhere else, or an odd-looking dark area all down one side.

IMPORTANT. *Before you start all the pieces of fabric must be clean and pressed.*

Crazy patchwork

Let's begin with this really easy form of patchwork. It's an excellent way to use up scraps of fabric that are rather small or are peculiar shapes. They probably wouldn't be any good for anything else. In addition to your patches you will need a piece of backing fabric that is the size of the completed shape (remember to add on the turnings allowance). This backing fabric should be of thinnish cotton – like a piece of an old sheet. If you make sure you finish off all the ends of thread neatly it can become the lining, with a kind of quilted effect.

Cut your patches out – any old shapes you like, but avoid curves. You'll have some bits like this:

Get a rough idea of the sort of arrangement you want by moving the patches around.

There are two basic methods of crazy patchwork, one where you have turnings and one where you don't.

The 'no turnings' method

Start in one corner. Pin a patch that has two sides forming a right angle on to one corner of the backing fabric. (We'll assume you are making a rectangular shaped piece of patchwork.) Don't turn the edges of the patch under.

Then build up the pattern by pinning the other patches on, overlapping the first one by at least 1·5cm. You can also slide some of the patches under others if they look better that way.

When you have pinned several patches on start the sewing. Don't sew right out to the edges of the backing fabric. Stop short, leaving the final turning allowance unstitched. If you have a machine with a swing needle you can use a very close zigzag stitch all around the edges. In one go this quickly completes the two jobs of joining the fabrics together and stopping the edges from fraying. One word of warning: you'll need rather a lot of thread – close zigzagging eats it up at an amazing rate.

If you are sewing by hand or using a straight-stitch machine sew the patches to the backing fabric with ordinary running stitch. These stitches should go through all the layers of fabric. Having sewn down the first few patches go on gradually pinning and sewing the rest of the patchwork.

Now you have to cover over the raw edges. There are several alternatives here. You can sew coloured tape or flat braid over the joins. Sew close to each edge of the tape or braid, not just along the centre as this wouldn't trap the fraying edges properly. On a patchwork made from heavy fabrics, such as woollen tweeds, strips of felt or suedette, cut out with pinking shears, can be used in the same way as the tape:

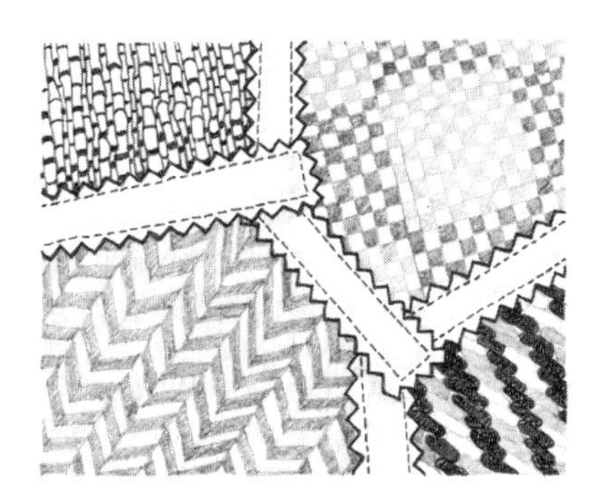

Another nice solution is to use wide rick-rack – that's this wiggly sort of braid:

A different way of covering and securing the raw edges is to do embroidery over them. Use blanket, herringbone or feather stitch (see pages 21, 161, 160) in a thickish thread. The type of fabrics used in the patchwork will suggest whether wool or cotton is best for the embroidery. If you are careful you can avoid letting the embroidery thread show on the back of the work by sewing only through the patches.

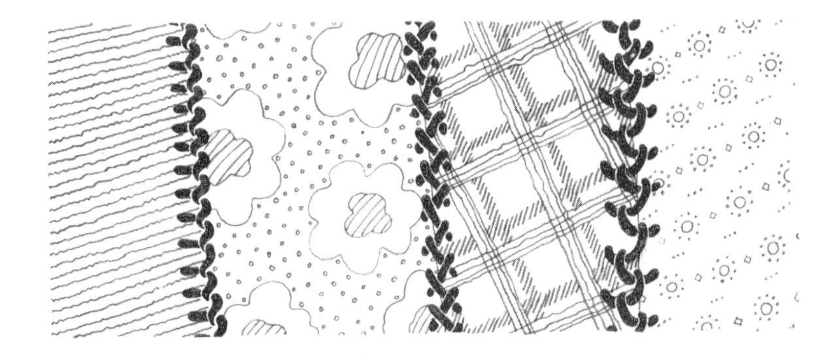

Finishing off. If you have managed to keep the back of your patchwork reasonably neat and it's not a mass of horrible loops and knots you can use it as a lining. The pattern of the stitches makes an interesting abstract quilted design.

Measure the piece of patchwork to see if all the sewing has made it slightly smaller than when it started life. If so, you'll have to reduce the final turnings around the edge to make the shape end up the right size. Turn the edges of the front under the right distance once and pin them. Turn the backing fabric under once, so that it is 5mm smaller all around than the front. This avoids the possibility of the lining showing by mistake. Sew the back and front together and finish off any details of embroidery, etc., that may need working out to the edges.

Where braid or something similar has been used to cover the joins a final edging of braid right round the piece would look great.

Don't worry if the back of your patchwork is rather a nasty-looking mess. You can conceal all the horrors beneath a lining. As described above, turn the lining piece under so that it is 5mm smaller all round than the front before sewing it on.

The 'with turnings' method

This technique is not suitable for very bulky fabrics because the turnings would be too thick and lumpy. As previously described, cut out a backing piece and the patches, but this time allow a little extra for turnings on each patch. There is no point in stipulating an exact amount for the turnings because you may not turn all the sides of a patch under. It depends how the patchwork develops. When sewing the patches on don't go right to the outside edges of the backing fabric. Leave the turning allowance free of stitches. Have the iron handy.

Begin the patchwork in just the same way as in the 'no turnings' method. Pin on the first patch, unturned, in one corner. On the edges of the patches that are to overlap this first one, iron down single 1cm turnings. Pin patches on in their overlapping positions. Sew down the overlapping edges of the patches with straight machining or, if you are hand sewing, use running stitch or hemming. Stitch as close to the turned edge as possible and sew right through the patches and the backing fabric. Work your way through the design, ironing the appropriate turnings under and pinning and sewing the patches on bit by bit until it's complete.

Finish the piece off by turning the front and back under as described in the previous section – 'Finishing off'. An attractive variation is to bind the edges with strips of one of the fabrics you've already used for patches. The thickness of your patchwork determines the width of the binding. The finished binding ends up one quarter of the width of the strip of binding you start with. For a patchwork of the cotton-sheet type of thickness make the binding 4cm wide. This will give a 1cm wide finished binding. Unless it's going to go round curves the binding doesn't need to be cut on the cross (diagonally). To avoid complications with corners, cut the binding to lengths 1cm longer than each edge to be bound. Iron under a tiny 5mm turning at each end of each binding strip. An easy way of sewing binding on by machine is like this. Pin the right side of the binding to the wrong side of the patchwork and sew it on 1cm down from the edge.

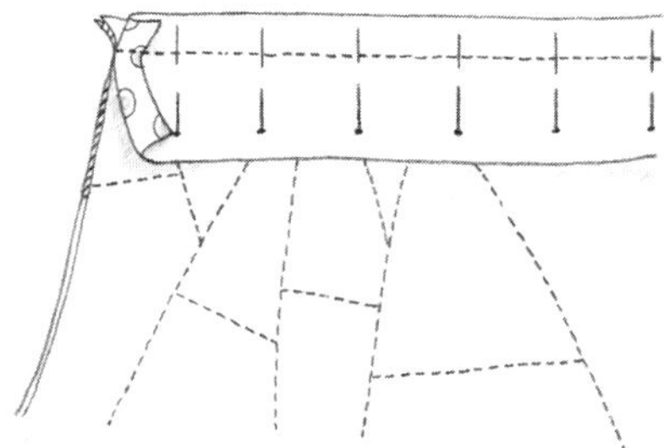

Turn the work over so that the right side of the patchwork is uppermost. Pull the binding over towards you and fold under a single 1cm turning along its edge. Pin the binding to the patchwork and sew it, by machine or by hand, as close to the edge of the binding as possible. You can also use braid, webbing or straight tape for binding. As these all have finished edges there's no need for double turning. The sewn binding comes out half the width of the original. Cut the braid to the required lengths plus 1cm. As previously described, iron under 5mm turnings at the raw ends. Carefully fold and iron the braid in half down its entire length (a damp cloth may be necessary here). Place the now V-sectioned binding astride the edge of the patchwork. Pin and tack it neatly down. Carefully machine or sew by hand close to the edge of the braid so that the stitches go through all the layers.

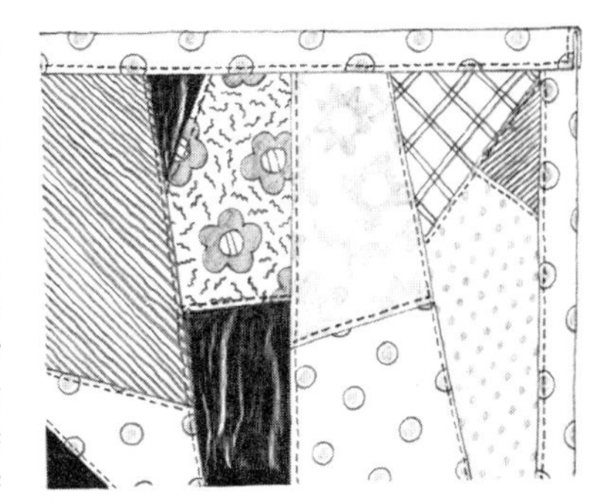

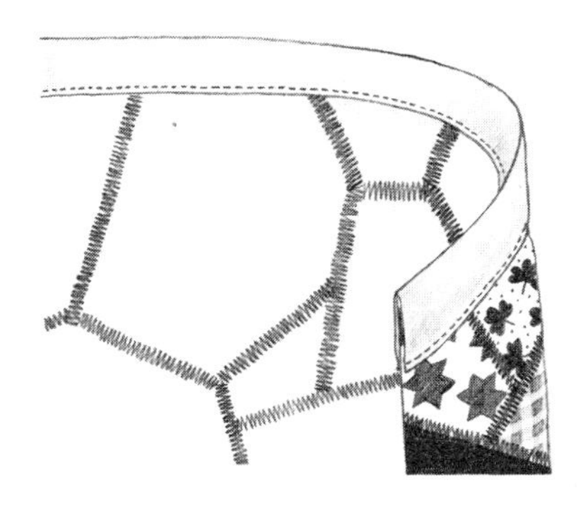

Squares, squares, squares

Although the actual making up of a patchwork of squares is easy enough you must be ACCURATE about how you cut the squares out and how you sew them together. Otherwise it will go all peculiar.

Decide upon the size you want the squares in the finished patchwork to be. Let's say, for example, you are going to make a rectangle 60 × 30cm comprising eighteen squares, each 10 × 10cm.

1	2	3	4	5	6
7	8	9	10	11	12
13	14	15	16	17	18

Using a set square to ensure your right angles actually are right angles, draw a 10 × 10cm square on a piece of card and cut it out. Now on a piece of paper draw and cut out another square which has 1·5cm added on each side for the turnings – in this case it will measure 13 × 13cm. Use this larger paper square as a pattern shape for your patches. Pin it to the different fabrics and cut out the number of squares you require. Cut out your squares on the grain of the fabric i.e. with the threads parallel to the edges of the square.

The smaller card square (10 × 10cm in this example) is used as a guide for the sewing lines. Lay each fabric square wrong side up and place the card square in the centre. Draw carefully all round the card square with a pencil or sharp tailor's chalk.

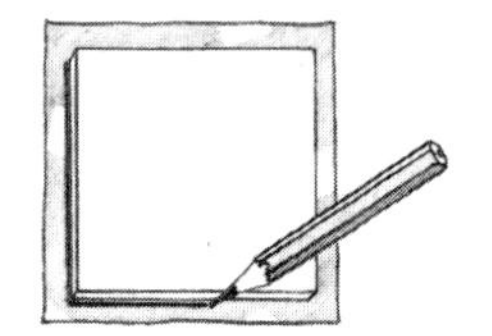

(Make sure it's sharp; you don't want a line 4mm thick.) If the fabric is too bumpy or quite unsuitable for drawing lines on you must adopt another approach. For this cut out a paper square the same size as the card one (10 × 10cm here). Pin it to the centre of the fabric square and run a quick line of tacking round it. Go right round the square as accurately as you can. Use a thread that shows up clearly against the colour of the material.

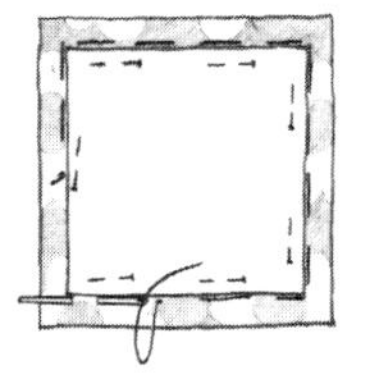

As with any patchwork, it makes sense to play around with the fabric squares at first, moving them about until you get the arrangement you like best.

You sew the patchwork squares into strips first. Start with the strip made up of squares 1 to 6. Take squares 1 and 2. Place their right sides together and put a couple of pins through the drawn lines so that the drawn lines lie exactly one on top of the other. You can keep looking at either side of the two squares to make sure the pins have come through in the right places. You are going to sew just one edge so put some more pins in at right angles like this along that edge:

Now machine or hand sew running stitch along the drawn line. In the same way, join on squares 3, 4, 5 and 6. Make up the other two strips, of squares 7 to 12 and 13 to 18. Then press all the seams open, nice and flat.

Now, using just the same idea, you join strip 1–6 to strip 7–12. Put the pins in lengthwise first to get the drawn lines to match up. Then pin all the way along at right angles and sew the strips together.

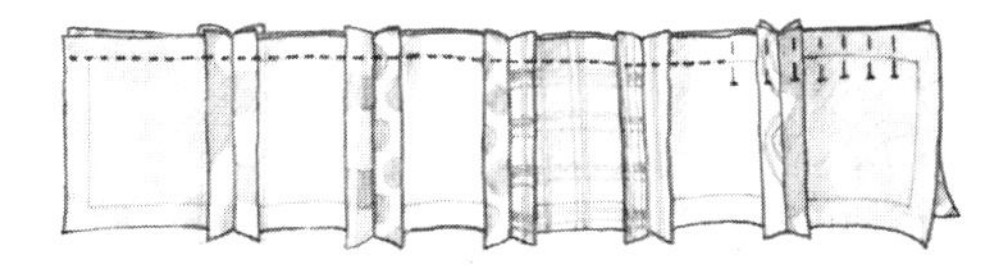

Sew on the final 12–18 strip, iron it all and the piece is completed.

You can apply exactly the same approach to a patchwork made up out of rectangular pieces.

If the patchwork is going to get a lot of wear and washing – as a piece made up from denims might do – you can make it extra strong by adding top stitching. First make sure it's all ironed properly. Then on the right side of the fabric run rows of stitching alongside all the seams, 4mm away from the actual seam line. This stitching goes through all the layers of material. On a denim patchwork in various shades and fades of blue this would look very dashing done in some contrasting colour like an orange or a brilliant green.

How about turning your squares patchwork round for a diagonal look?

Patchwork from old woollies

Knitted sweaters, cardigans, scarves and tops become unwearable for a variety of reasons. They shrink. They stretch. They go baggy. They suddenly acquire mysterious moth holes. They get things spilt on them. Or they just simply wear out. However far gone they are, there are always some bits that will do for patchwork.

Knitting, like weaving, is a way of making yarn into fabric. For patchworking you treat the knitting as a piece of cloth. In some countries it is the standard practice to knit up pieces, especially tubes, and then cut them into shapes and sew the shapes together to make garments.

There are loads of different types of wools and man-made yarns used in knitting. Be sure you use patches of similar weight and thickness in your patchwork piece. Hand-knitted pure wool gives the most luxurious patchwork. Providing the knitting is of the same sort of weight you can combine hand- and machine-knitted woollen patches. For cosy warmth make a delicious thick patchwork from heavy ribbing, bits of Aran sweater and chunky knitting. Pieces of finer knitting would combine to make a lighter-weight garment – still warm though. You'll need to line the patchwork – use a slightly stretchy material like cotton jersey.

Wash the woollies first. Use a fabric conditioner because it revives the texture of the wool and you might as well give your old sweaters all the help they can get. When they are dry cut open the seams and press all the pieces. Use a damp cloth and iron on the wrong side of the knitting. Now you can see exactly what you've got – which bits are usable and which should be discarded.

Squares or rectangles

The basic instructions for making up a patchwork of squares or rectangles are given on page 125. There are just one or two points that apply specifically to knitted pieces.

Pin your paper pattern on so that it lies parallel with the rows of stitching, not at an angle. Carefully cut round the shape. Don't panic – it's not all going to unravel and ladder like mad.

You can't draw on the knitting unless it's very fine, so use the tacking method to mark out the sewing lines. (See page 126.) Machine the patches together – straight stitch – or, if hand sewing, use backstitching. If machining, watch that the machine foot doesn't get snared up in the knitting. When you've finished your woolly patchwork iron all the seams flat (damp cloth) and line the piece, or alternatively line it when it is incorporated in a garment.

Knitted squares

Remember those squares that people used to knit or crochet to sew together to make blankets? Maybe you've even got some poked away somewhere in a cupboard. You put them there feeling slightly ashamed of the fact that, in spite of all your efforts, you still seemed acres away from a blanket. Knitted or crocheted squares or rectangles are ideal to make into patchwork for clothing – especially as the edges are all nicely finished off. You join one square to another by oversewing by hand or zigzagging on a machine.

It's a great way of using up odd, otherwise useless, bits of wool. There's no reason why a square should be just in one colour. It can be striped to use up really tiny amounts of wool. It's very satisfying when you complete a square quite quickly, even if you're not much good at knitting or crochet. With gentle persuasion you might be able to get the whole family going on it. (For how to unpick sweaters, etc., and get the wool back into excellent knittable condition, see page 14.)

Crazy patches

Cut-up sweaters make stylish crazy patchwork. Knitting has a slight tendency to start to come unravelled when you cut it at an angle, away from the straight. However, providing you handle the pieces carefully and don't let the cat play with them, all will be well. You can use the 'no turnings' method (it's all explained on page 121) by butting one piece of knitting up against the next, not overlapping them. This type of crazy patchwork is particularly effective in thick chunky knitting.

Cut the shapes as you go along, making sure that they fit together. It's rather like making up a jigsaw puzzle. Pin and then sew them to the backing fabric with straight machine-stitching or by hand with back-stitch. When they are all attached cover all the seams with the braid method. Use braid, tape or cut felt or suede-type strips that are wide enough to cover across the joins adequately and prevent any loose ends of wool escaping. On thick woollens this gives a lovely quilted result that looks as if it cost a fortune. Embroidery doesn't work as a finishing-off technique in this case, because it doesn't cover the joins well enough. When it's dirty, dry-clean, rather than wash, this type of patchwork.

The 'with turnings' approach is best suited to thinner bits of knitting. Cut the crazy patches out and, using a damp cloth, iron under the single turnings. Sew all the patches on to the backing fabric with straight machining or hand-sewn backstitch. Complete the patchwork by embroidering over the joins in wool of a contrasting colour (or colours) with any of the three embroidery stitches – buttonhole, herringbone or feather stitch. If you don't know how to do them, turn to page 160, where all is revealed.

NOTE. *Never try using an iron-on method for patchwork techniques that use braid. The braid is not merely a trimming but part of the actual structure of the fabric, so it needs to be sewn for strength.*

Quilting

Quilted fabric is warm and light and can be used in all sorts of ways. It's lovely and cosy, which means you can look bright and cheerful during the coldest weather.

Ready-made quilted material is very expensive to buy. But you can make your own by recycling various fabrics. The modern quiltings on sale use man-made wadding and you can buy this by the metre if you want to. It comes in several thicknesses but a thin one is normally the most suitable for using in clothes. On the other hand, like the old American pioneers, you can use up old blankets – even if they are a bit worn – for the cosy part. Another suggestion is to cut up and use an old quilted dressing gown. Don't unpick the quilting, just use it as it is. In addition to whatever you are using for wadding you'll need some thin cloth as a backing – something like a piece of sheet or curtain lining would do. The fabric you use for the top, the layer that's on show, should be lightweight and closely woven. Lightweight cottons or synthetics are suitable. If you are adding some quite small areas of quilting to a garment (as in the shirt-jacket on page 90) you could achieve a most luxurious effect by using an old silk scarf or a fine woollen one.

You make a piece of quilting and then cut out the shapes you require.

With a ruler and nice sharp tailor's chalk measure and draw out the grid pattern that you are going to sew. Draw this on the right side of the top fabric. Start off with a grid pattern of squares or diamonds for your first efforts, whilst you are still getting the hang of it. Squares 3·5 × 3·5cm would be a suitable size.

Sandwich the wadding or blanket between the backing cloth and the top fabric. How many layers of blanket you use depends upon the state of your blanket and how the quilting is being used. Two thicknesses of a rather old blanket should be sufficient for quilting used in clothing. Tack all the layers of fabric together so that they don't slide around.

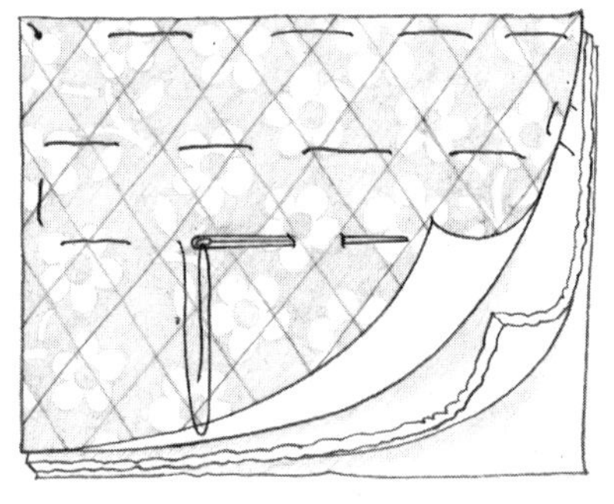

It is possible to sew quilting by hand but it is very laborious, especially doing lots of straight lines of tiny stitches. So if you haven't a machine, try to get the use of one for this job. See the end of this chapter for some special hand-sewing ideas.

When machining a piece of quilting it's a good plan to do a little test bit first. This will show you if you need to adjust the tension at all. Having sorted that out, you simply machine along all your guide-lines right through all the layers. The backing fabric now becomes a lining. The piece of quilting is now ready for you to use as you wish.

To make a neat finish, whether you are applying a piece of quilting to a garment or making up a quilted item, bind the edges. Use home-made binding in, say, a contrasting print or colour. (It tells you how to do binding like this on page 124.)

Quilted skirt

You can work a quilted section on to a garment like this skirt. Sandwich the wadding or blanket strip between the skirt material and the backing fabric. Allow an extra 3cm turning along the top edge of the backing fabric and a 5cm turning for the bottom hem on the skirt. Tack all the layers together first, as usual, and machine the quilting lines. When that's finished, double turn and sew the backing fabric turning and the skirt hem to conceal any raw edges. A finishing touch is a line of russia braid along the top edge of the quilted part, repeated again on the waistband (or wherever else you feel like). In a fabric with a small-scale flowery print this looks like a traditional south-of-France type skirt. Think how you could revive a tired old skirt in navy cotton by quilting it in red – possible using a double thread (page 107). Trimmings in bright red russia braid would complete it.

Further ideas

Quilting in parallel lines is very effective but make the lines quite close – about 2cm apart, perhaps.

Try machining your quilting with a weird pattern of wiggly lines or zigzags. Anything will do. But keep the lines of sewing distributed evenly over the quilting. You don't want to end up with great patches of nothing in some parts and dense masses of squiggles elsewhere. Have a go at some pictures too. You can draw the design in tailor's chalk before sewing it but don't make it too complicated!

Patchwork

Quilted patchwork looks good if you follow the pattern made by the joins. Patchwork done in lightweight cottons or similar fabrics is best. Tack together the backing fabric, the wadding or blanket and the patchwork (which is the top fabric). Machine along the seamlines of the patchwork, through all the layers. If you use huge patches you'll have to quilt over them too, not just along the seams.

Crazy patching and quilting

In one operation you can make a piece of crazy patchwork that is quilted too. Tack the backing fabric and the wadding or blanket together. Use lightweight cotton or something equivalent for the crazy patches. Follow the technique explained on page 123 for the 'with turnings' method. As you sew on each patch your stitches go right through the patches, the wadding and the backing fabric. Imagine how gorgeous a waistcoat of crazy quilting made from cut-up old silk ties would look!

All done by hand

For a really dramatic effect try hand sewing some giant-sized quilting with huge plain stitches in embroidery cotton or silk. Just tack your three layers of fabric together as previously explained and, with a huge needle, sew in and out through all three layers.

Decorating

Design ideas

From here on in this book you'll find various techniques explaining how to individualize and decorate your clothes. These include stick-on and sew-on decoration, embroidery, pattern dyeing, fabric painting and printing. Give some of your old favourites a new look or make some clothes deliberately designed to be decorated. (It's surprising how chic a length of old sheeting can become.)

Certain of the processes, like some forms of tie and dye and printing, automatically produce their own images or patterns. All you have to do there is to arrange them in the best-looking places. In other cases the decoration needs to be based on some sort of design.

Now, you will have no problem at all in thinking up designs and ways of applying them if you are a budding Picasso. But, just in case you're not, and you've got that sinking 'can't draw' feeling, here are a few suggestions about using decoration and some thoughts on where you can find ideas for designs.

Borders and edges

You can always go round the edge of anything. Frequently, of necessity, you have to sew the edge to finish off a garment – so why not make this fancy sewing? And then you can go round again inside that line of sewing, echoing it with, perhaps, another colour and/or another technique. Go on and on, if you like, and fill up every available bit of space. Lots of telephone pad doodlings do this. Just try some and you'll find you can develop all sorts of patterns.

Geometric patterns

Experiment with pencil, ruler, compasses and set square. Plan an arrangement, on paper, which will, at this stage, just be in lines. Don't waste time colouring it in. You do that later on when you transfer it to the garment.

Paper with squares printed on it is useful for working out designs too. If you have no printed paper fold a piece of plain paper up carefully over and over again. Open it out and the creases act as the dividing lines between the squares.

Adding your own design to ready-patterned fabrics

This idea works very sucessfully on a material that's printed or woven with a geometric pattern – stripes, checks, spots – that sort of thing. The existing pattern forms a grid and you can fill in any sections of the grid you wish. Try different coloured cross-stitch on the squares of a printed check. Cheer up a stripy top by printing along the white stripes.

Letters and numbers

Initials, names and numbers are all good design material. Look for, and copy or trace, attractive letter styles in magazines or on record sleeves.

Familiar surroundings

Think of the things around you: your house, your friends, your family, your own face, your pet cat, your dog, your goldfish, your gerbil, your hyena (hyena?). You're so used to them that you really hardly notice them any more. Have a go at drawing them – that'll make you look at them properly. If it doesn't come out right the first time don't fling the pencil out of the window and kick the telly. National Gallery material is not required. All you need is the beginning of an idea to transfer on to the piece of clothing. Once you get going with whichever technique you choose you'll find the actual doing of the technique takes over and the original drawing was only a starting-point anyway.

Have a close look at some leaves, flowers or seed-heads and work out how they are constructed. Generally they are symmetrical, i.e. one half is an exact replica of the other. Use thin paper and fold it down the middle. Draw one half of the object on one side of the fold and trace the other half through on to the other side.

Other everyday things can spark off ideas. Look around the kitchen. Someone somewhere has designed the label on the strawberry jam, the packet of tea, the box of matches and the tin of cat food. Borrow bits and pieces from these designs. See if there are any usable motifs on the paper tissues box, on your iced lolly wrapper, printed on your dinner plates or woven into the hearth-rug. Get ideas from books, greeting cards, wrapping paper and magazines – both from drawings and photographs.

How to alter the size of a design

Occasionally you are lucky and you can just trace a design but all too often the picture in a book or your own drawing is the wrong size. There is a simple way of enlarging it called squaring up.

Paper-clip a piece of tracing paper over the design. Draw a rectangle round the motif, in this case the owl, literally touching the edges of it. Trace the owl.

Now, on a piece of paper big enough for your final design, draw two sides of a rectangle in the top left-hand corner. Call these lines AB and AC. Clip your tracing over this, lining up AB and AC with the corresponding lines at the top left-hand corner of the owl rectangle. Draw a diagonal right through the owl rectangle and on across the plain paper.

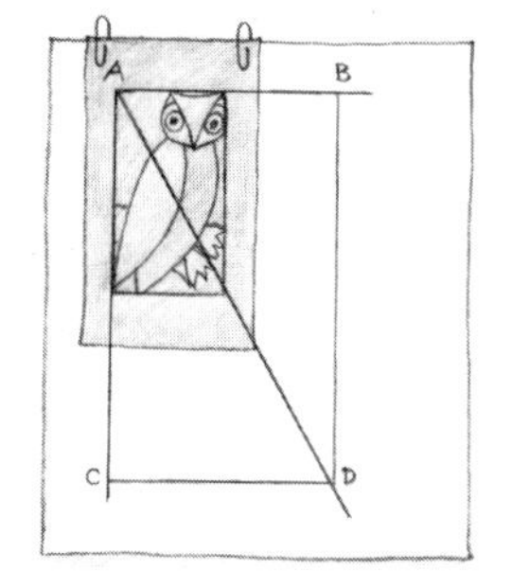

Decide how big you want the new owl to be and make a rectangle to contain it by drawing a line at a right angle from AB down to the diagonal and another line at a right angle from AC across to the diagonal to meet at D. This new rectangle is bigger but in the same proportion as the original owl rectangle.

Go back to the owl tracing and, with your ruler, divide the rectangle into quarters first. Halve these so that you get a grid of sixteen little rectangles all over it. Do exactly the same thing with rectangle ABDC – divide that into sixteen smaller rectangles.

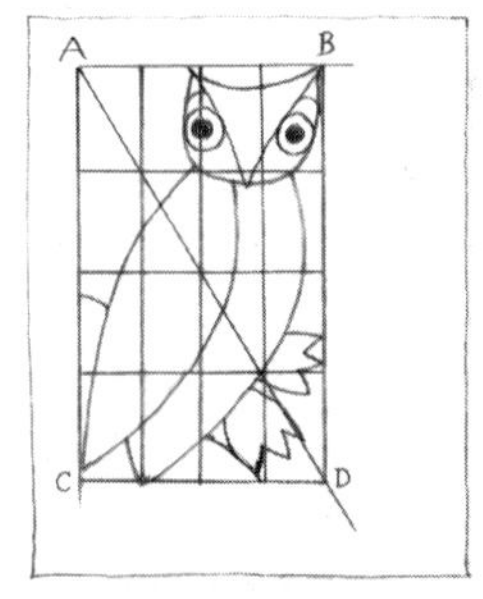

Now it's easy to copy the design from the smaller grid to the larger one because you can see where each part of the owl comes in each of the grid rectangles.

Exactly the same principle can be used to reduce the size of a design.

How to transfer a design on to fabric

Whichever method of decoration you are going to use, you will first need to convey the design out of your head and on to the fabric in outlines. You can draw it straight on with tailor's chalk (rather than pencil, which is difficult to remove later). Another way is to draw the design on some thinnish paper and then go over the lines on the back of the paper with chalk. With the pencil drawing uppermost, pin the paper in the right position to the cloth. Go over the lines again with pencil. This will transfer a chalk outline on to the cloth ready for you to start work. One word of warning – make sure the material is stretched out taut when you do this. Pin or sticky tape it out flat on the table.

The great jacket saga

Consider what you can do by combining lots of ways of decorating clothing. This jacket is like an extra-special autograph album. It's been passed around a group of friends, each of whom has added his or her contribution – painted, embroidered, sewn-on, etc. Try it with something of your own. Or make a decorative diary – all over your jeans, perhaps. Record the things and events you want to remember in embroidery, appliqué, printing and so on. Something to pass on to your great-great-grandchildren!

Dye laughing

Dyeing clothes is dead easy and it's cheap too. Brighten up your old drabbies with new colours. Things that are too good to discard – not worn out but excessively boring – can be transformed. Re-vitalize dull old shirts and sweaters. A new colour will work wonders on last year's T-shirts and dresses. Quite an ordinary dress becomes surprisingly sophisticated when worn with clever colour-matching scarf and tights.

Think of all those Christmas presents hats and gloves, lovingly knitted by kind aunties. They just don't go with anything. A quick whirl in the dye – and you have some stylish accessories. Everybody in the land must surely confess to having the odd article of yellowish-grey underwear tucked away somewhere. Fish them out and include them in your next dyeing session. You'll have dashing bras and pants fit to parade on the beach.

Extract every bit of colour from your dye mix. Pop in old zips, buttons, ribbons and trimmings – they will all come in handy. (Some buttons won't, in fact, dye – but you can't tell without trying.)

The range of dyes on display in the shops may look a bit daunting.

First establish what type of fabric the things you want to dye are made of. Nowadays the garment label will tell you this but older things may not carry such information. If you are unsure try asking a craft or needlework teacher or the shop assistant on the dye counter. If you simply can't identify the type of fabric cut off a piece that doesn't matter (a narrow strip from inside the hem, for instance) and see if this will take the dye.

If you have a mixture of, say, woollen, nylon and polyester items you probably won't be able to dye them all together. Different types of dye work on different types of fabric. Some use cold and some hot water.

WARNING! *There are just a few man-made fibre fabrics that you cannot dye at home. Shops have charts explaining all this but, if in doubt, do ask the assistant.*

DON'T *dye swimwear. The chlorine in swimming pools can have a very nasty effect on home-dyeing.*

You must weigh the things to be dyed so that you will know how much dye to buy. Do this when they are dry, not wet. Weigh all the woollen things together and write down the weight, weigh all the nylon things together and so on.

Select the dye appropriate to your fabric and then choose the colour.

Here are a few basic facts about colours:

White or very pale things can be dyed to any colour.

All colours will dye to black but they won't all come out exactly the same kind of black.

You can't dye a colour to a lighter colour, only to a stronger or darker one.

Dye will not completely cover the original colour of a garment unless it was very pale. The original colour will blend with the new dye colour just like paints do when you mix them together. For instance, a yellow T-shirt dyed blue will come out green.

Any colour can successfully be dyed a darker version of itself: for example a bright red like scarlet can be dyed to a darker red like crimson. Of course there are all sorts of variations in colours. The darkness or the lightness of a blue, or the fact that it is a greeny blue, will influence the colour to which you dye it.

You can get some most sophisticated results by dyeing material that is already patterned. A blue and white checked shirt dyed orange comes out brown where the blue was and orange where it was white – very elegant. A bright flowery-patterned skirt that you are really fed up with becomes much more grown up when you dye it olive green. The flowers are still there but in subtle muted browns and greens.

If you intend to make a patterned garment, either out of new material or by converting something, try dyeing a piece of the fabric before you make it up. It's really smart to team the same fabric design in two (or more) different colourways.

This is a general guide as to what can be dyed what:

Original Colour of Fabric +	*Dye* =	*Resulting New Colour*
White or very pale colour	Any colour	Any colour
Any colour	Black	Black, but the original colour will influence it – so you will get blueish blacks, brownish blacks, etc.
Any colour	A darker version of the original colour	A darker version of the original colour
With any of the following you can swap 'original colour' with 'dye' to give the same result.		
Red	Yellow	Orange
Red	Blue	Purple or brownish-purple
Yellow	Blue	Green or olive
Yellow	Purple	Brown, ochre or grey
Blue	Orange	Brown or greenish-grey
Orange	Green	Grey or yellowish-brown
Green	Red	Brown
Purple	Orange	Grey or rust

Getting on with it

So you've selected the right type of dye for your material and you have bought the correct quantity in your chosen colour. Now to do and dye.

The garments to be dyed must be clean. Remove any stains too. Although your dye may be a strong colour it's no good hoping great blobs left by carelessly flung tomato sauce will simply disappear.

Before you begin read the dye manufacturer's instructions thoroughly. Don't just skim through them because you are keen to get started – actually sit down and study them. Dreary though this may seem, it does prevent disaster. Get all the equipment and ingredients ready first so that you don't have to rush round the house dripping Midnight Purple everywhere whilst you hunt out the measuring jug.

Always wear rubber gloves when dyeing (unless you fancy blue hands for a week or two) and wear an overall too. Lay newspaper over your working surface. A plastic bucket will do for cold-water dyeing but for hot-water dye you will need a non-leaking, heatproof metal container such as a preserving pan, metal bucket or large saucepan. Hot-water dye has to simmer on the cooker. You will also require a stick for stirring. To avoid accidental splashes spread newspaper on the floor around the cooker.

Dyeing in a washing-machine

For large items or a batch of things all to be dyed the same colour you can use a washing-machine. BUT – a cautionary word – obviously you are going to make some enemies if you rush in to do your dyeing and in the process turn the washing-machine and the greater part of the kitchen Mexican Orange; GET PERMISSION to use the machine for this. Again, read the directions properly. Some machines will not run cold and are therefore only suitable for hot water dyes. Check this first.

As instructed, only half load the machine. If you stuff it full everything will come out patchy. When you have finished, remove your dyed items and let the machine run through its cycle with very hot water, detergent and bleach to remove all traces of dye.

Dye patterns

So far we've only considered plain dyeing, just changing the colour of something all over. Now let's see how you can dye things so that you get patterns on them.

Obviously, with all these decorative dyeing techniques, the same basic principles outlined in the previous chapter apply. You must use the correct dye for your particular fabric and the right quantity of it. However, the fabrics you are going to use for these types of craft dyeing must be light in weight. Try to use cotton fabrics. These could be recycled cotton lawn, poplin, cheesecloth, sheeting or lining. If you're lucky enough to find any, silk would be fabulous. The reason why cotton and silk are recommended is that cold-water dyes can be used with them. When you are fiddling about with tying, dipping and the various techniques it makes things a great deal easier if your dye is merely sitting there ready for you and doesn't have to be heated up.

By the way, once cold dyes are mixed with water, providing you haven't added the fixer, you can store them in sealed jars in a dark cupboard for a few weeks. This means there's no mad panic to finish all your pattern dyeing in one afternoon!

Some garments, either because of their shape or because of the fabric from which they are made, are clearly unsuitable for pattern dyeing. You'd be hard put to fold and dip a hacking jacket, for example. So use your head and go for lightweight garments or pieces of material to make up after you've dyed them.

There are a number of methods of preventing the dye from reaching all the parts of the fabric. This automatically produces the pattern. The most straightforward way is fold and dip.

Fold and dip

You fold the material in, for example, accordion pleats, clip it with clothes pegs to stop it all falling apart and simply dip the edges of the folds into the dye.

Keeping it horizontal, hang it up to dry somewhere where the drips don't matter. When you undo it you will have a pattern like this:

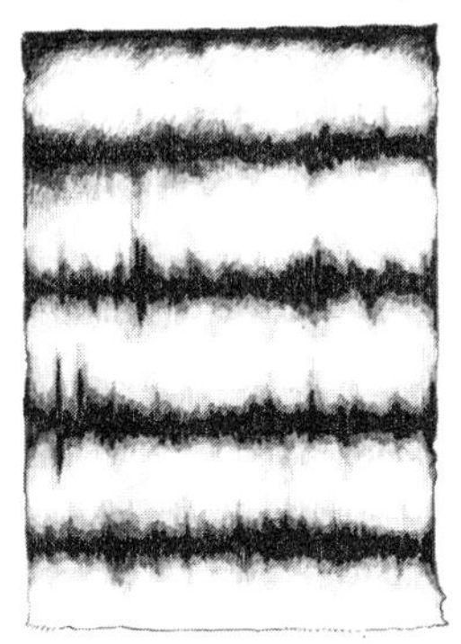

Rinse the fabric to remove any excess dye. Dampening the fabric before dipping it makes the dye run more over the material. It also gives it a paler, more misty effect.

If you folded it carefully, using an iron to make the pleats, you could dye this pattern round the bottom of a summer skirt or dress.

Some more fold and dip suggestions

Accordion pleat and dip the fabric just as before. Then swap the clothes pegs round so that they grip the dyed edges. Dip the undyed edges into another colour dye. Result – a two-colour stripe.

Dye stripes by the accordion-pleat method and let the fabric dry. Then create a check by pleating across the other way and dipping again.

For this:

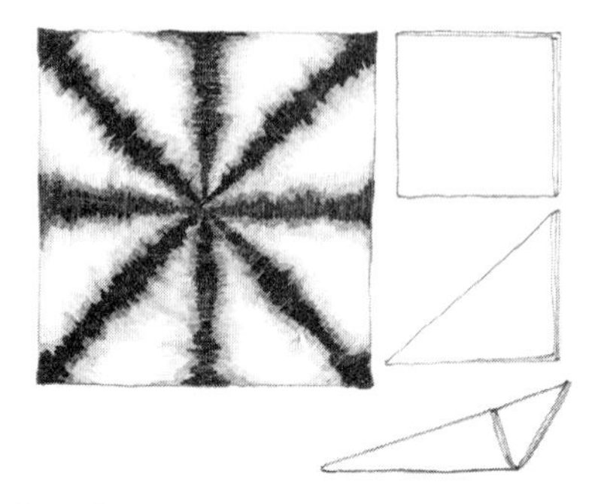

fold the square in four first to make a quarter-sized square and then fold that into a triangle, and again into a narrower triangle. Dip the bottom edges.

Experiment by folding pieces of soft toilet paper or paper towels into different patterns and dipping the edges into the dye. Being absorbent, this type of paper shows you the sort of result you'll get on the cloth.

A lovely idea, which you can apply to all these pattern dyeing processes, is to dye an experimental square (or squares) of cloth each time you are trying a technique. Later these can all be sewn together into a fantastic patchwork. Have a look at page 64.

Tie and dye

With this method you create a pattern on your cloth by tying it up tightly so that the dye cannot penetrate to the heart of the tied-up bits. You have to use string or thread that's dye-resistant, otherwise the dye just goes straight through it. Nylon string or bead thread, fishing line, elastic bands and plastic-coated wire are all excellent things to use for tying. Leave a short length of string or thread at the start so that you've something to tie the final end to – and do tie your knots TIGHTLY.

Marbling

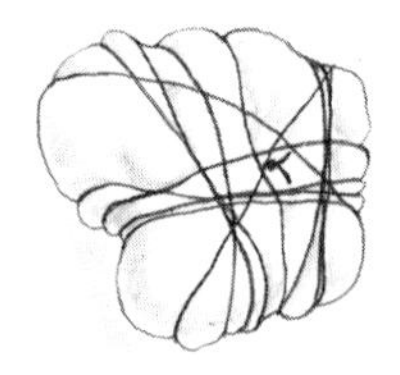

This gives a pattern very like some kinds of real marble. Screw the material up and tie it into a tight, hard ball by winding string or elastic bands round in different directions. Thoroughly wet the cloth ball. Now immerse it in the dye, for whatever length of time the manufacturers recommend, stirring it around as directed. That done, remove it and place it in clean water. Cut the ties, being very careful not to cut the fabric with the points of the scissors. Rinse the material again. If you want to, you can re-crumple the fabric and dye it once more in another colour.

As this is a random irregular pattern, which you can keep adding to by re-dyeing, you can use it on quite a large garment such as a dress or a shirt.

Get knotted

Lift up the centre of a piece of cloth, as with this square scarf and tie it in a knot; dye it – and you get this beautiful flower-like design.

Several knots in a line give an uneven stripy effect as on this wrap-around skirt.

Stoned

Tie a clean stone into the cloth and wind the string round it a few times in different directions. Then bind the fabric tightly at intervals away from the stone. So you'll have an object that resembles this:

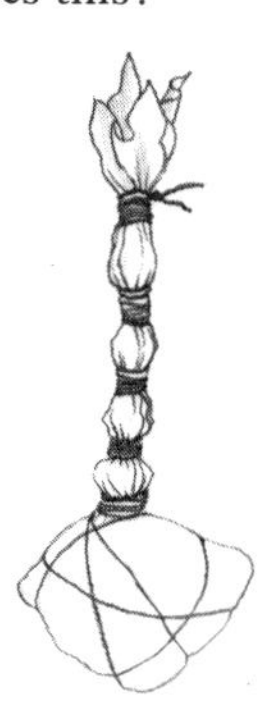

When it's dyed it makes a pattern of irregular circles within one another as on the vest below.

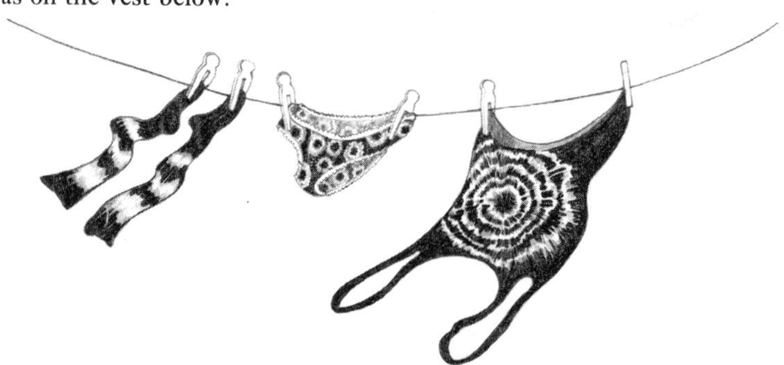

For an all-over pattern tie in lots of little stones or other objects that won't melt in the dye – like buttons, marbles, acorns, etc. If you're very painstaking use loads of fiddly little things, such as dried peas, tied in with fine thread, to make beautiful delicate spotty designs.

The sunburst

Dramatic sunburst patterns are easy to do. Lift up a piece of the cloth, twist it into a point and bind it tightly. Now it's ready to dye. This is the kind of motif that you get:

Tritik

This is a technique of pattern dyeing where tightly gathered-up stitching is used to keep the dye at bay. You need a strong thread because it's under considerable strain when you pull it up. Fishing line, buttonhole or carpet thread are all suitable. To get the idea, try a small experimental piece of fabric first, say a triangular scarf (they make super presents).

Tie a knot in your thread about 15cm from the end. This is to give you enough thread to get hold of when you want to tie up the gathering later. Sew some lines, squares, or wiggles in running stitch. You don't have to sew particularly neatly. When you get to the end of a line of stitching once again leave at least 15cm of thread. Don't do any gathering up until all the sewing is finished.

Take the odd tuck in the material and oversew it. You'll have something that looks like this at this stage:

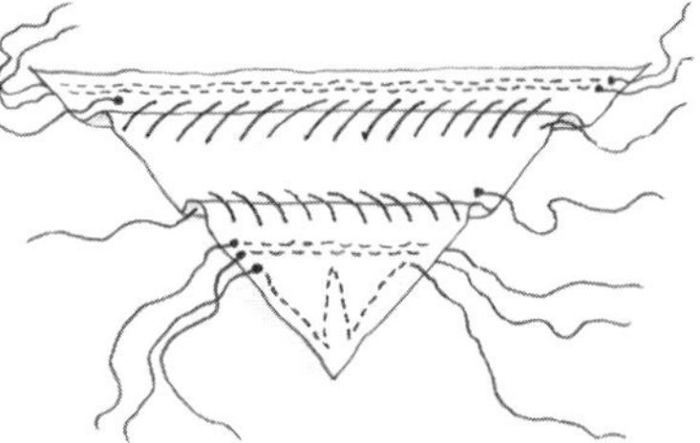

Then pull the loose ends of each line of stitching up as tightly as you can and knot them firmly to one another so that you've got a funny little screwed-up lump of rag. Wet this and then dye it in the usual way. After the final rinsing, carefully cut and pull out the threads.

Once you've experimented and found out the unique designs tritik will produce, go on to greater things. Imagine delicate tritik worked on the bust of a white smock, then dyed blue. The weird spidery pattern would come out in white and shades of blue on the bust, the rest of the smock would be solid blue.

Another idea – big leafy shapes done in tritik on an exotic shawl.

Batik

Dye won't go through wax. If you put melted wax on to fabric it penetrates right through the cloth; when the fabric is dyed all the wax-covered bits remain the original colour. This technique is called batik. It's a fascinating hobby and (as with all these pattern dyeing methods) it doesn't matter a bit whether you can draw or not – you can still produce your own individual fabrics. The shirred skirt and top photographed on page 41 are batiked – no particular design, just a lot of enjoyable splodging around on what started life as a very ordinary length of plain white lining.

Cold-water dyes are essential for batik (otherwise the wax would start melting when you didn't want it to). For the wax, ordinary white candles will do, but, if you can get any, the addition of a little beeswax is recommended because candle wax alone is rather brittle and inclined to crack off. Beeswax is sold in ironmongers, chemists and craft shops, but do-it-yourselfers often have a chunk hidden away in the shed.

Try batik out first on a smallish piece of material to see how it's done. Here's the equipment you will need: a couple of cheap paste or paint brushes, one fat and one thin, and some sort of frame to stretch the fabric across with drawing-pins. This can be an old picture frame or the open top of a big cardboard carton. Don't work with your fabric laid flat on the table because the wax will stick it down firmly to the table top! Arrange to work at a table covered in newspaper (to catch any drips) next to the cooker where you are going to melt the wax. There are two important reasons for this: firstly, wandering around the kitchen dripping hot wax is a rotten idea and, secondly, the wax cools extraordinarily quickly so you must work near the heat source.

Have a nice sturdy saucepan with some water constantly simmering away. Put the wax into a tin or small pot (*not* a plastic carton like a yoghurt cup – it could melt) and stand it in the simmering water to melt down and remain liquid. (It's not unlike cooking a steamed pud.) The wax is too hot if it starts to smoke, so turn it down. It's just right if, when you paint some on the fabric, it looks like a grease mark. This means that it has gone right through the material. If it looks white on the fabric it's too cool and is only coating the top side of the cloth – so the dye will sneak in round the back.

If you want to have a go at a design draw it lightly on your fabric with tailor's chalk. Remember the bits that are going to be covered by wax stay undyed so it's rather like making a negative. Usually you draw or paint in the dark parts of a design. Here you paint the light areas.

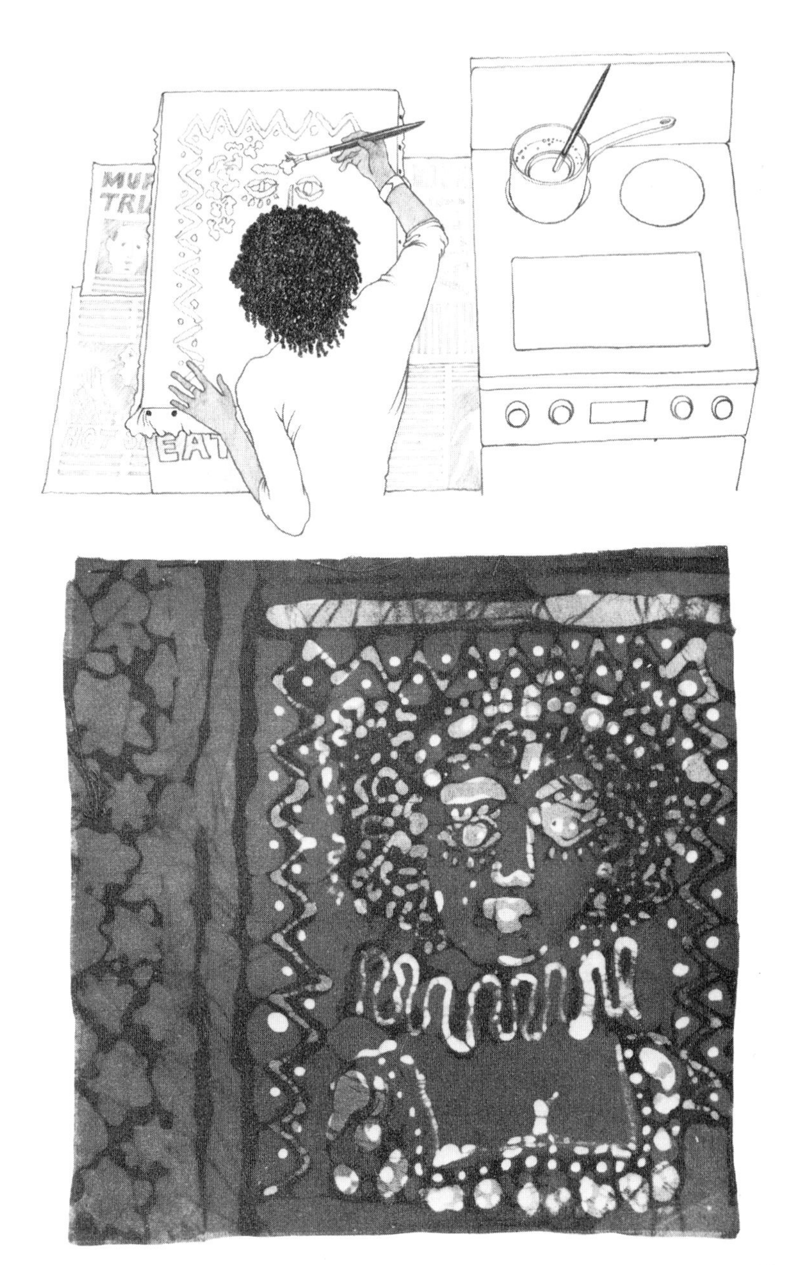

Because the molten wax cools so quickly as you take a brushful from the pot to your fabric you must paint rapidly. It's no good being fussy and niggly. Accept any accidental blobs and enjoy sloshing it around. Try outlines of dots and splashes by letting the brush drip as you pass it over the cloth.

When you think you've done enough turn off the cooker. Keep the brushes in the wax (which will quickly go solid) as they are only really suitable for batiking now.

Unpin your fabric. Screwing it up a bit encourages the waxed areas to crackle. The dye will penetrate these cracks and give the fine cobwebby lines that are typical of batik work.

Now dye the fabric with a cold-water dye, rinse it and hang it up to dry.

To remove the wax from the cloth lay a thick pad of newspaper on the table and then sandwich your batik between two layers of paper towels or some similar absorbent plain paper. Iron it with a hot iron to draw the wax out of the fabric into the paper. Keep changing the paper as it gets waxy. If you use newspaper for this there is a danger of the printing coming off on to your batik. Get rid of any final wax marks by washing the material in hot water and detergent.

Multi-colour batik

Imagine you have a rather uninteresting pale pink shirt – comfortable, useful – but how dull can you get? Try out multi-colour batik on it and turn it into something special.

Wax paint your design and then dye the shirt red. If you removed the wax at this stage you would have a pink and red shirt.

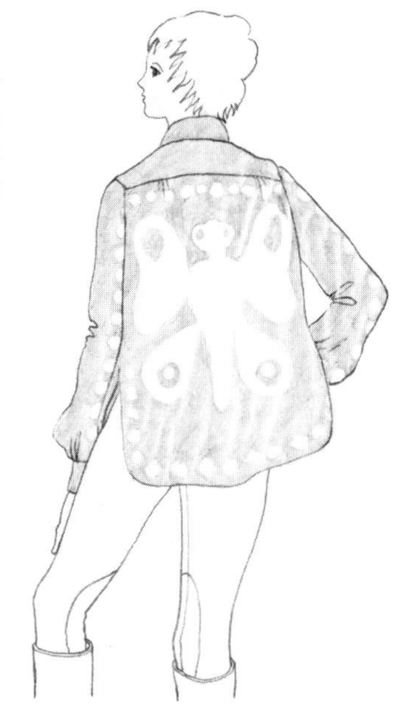

Now paint on new wax, in some places over the pink parts and in other places over the red parts. Re-dye the shirt in blue, dry it and remove the wax.

Some of the shirt will remain pink, having been protected by wax during both dyeings. Other bits, formerly pink but this time exposed to the blue dye, will turn blue. A third colour, purple, will appear where the blue dyed over the red bits. You could go on adding and combining colours as much as you liked.

Another approach is to let the fabric dry after the first dyeing, then paint on more wax areas. This, however, gives less opportunity for unusual and exciting colour combinations to occur.

Embroidery

Embroidery. Does the very word dismay you? Weedy little daisies lurking in the corner of tablecloths? Fear not. Embroidery, having been rather ill, has come to life again. No longer must it take for ever to finish a piece. You can get some stunning effects by using a few really simple stitches in marvellous colours. Embroider on anything you like and add anything you like – beads, buttons, ribbons, fur, bits of appliqué . . . anything.

Yarns, threads, etc.

First, what can you use to embroider with that won't cost you the earth? The silks, cottons and wools sold specifically for embroidery, in rather small hanks, work out very expensive if you are thinking of covering a large area. Become, if you are not already, a yarn and wool hoarder. Page 14 offers advice on acquiring wool cheaply, de-crinkling it if you're undoing a knitted garment and dyeing it.

Dishcloth cotton (intended, strange to relate, for knitting dishcloths) can be bought in balls of approximately 150 metres. It's a nice soft cotton, about the thickness of parcel-type string, and very similar to the cotton sold especially for embroidery. It comes only in a slightly off-white colour, but, as it works out much much cheaper than embroidery cotton, you may consider it worth buying some and dyeing it to the colours of your choice. (Remember, you don't have to dye one item at a time. This might be a good opportunity to dye a lot of bits and pieces that have been hanging about for ages waiting for the big colour change.)

Hand embroidery stitches

Here a few basic hand embroidery stitches are explained, with some suggestions as to how they might be used. Once you get going you'll want to try all sorts of combinations of your own. If you do become fascinated by it, search the library for books on the embroidery of the different countries of the world and on further techniques. Our museums contain wonderful examples for you to see too.

Running stitch

This has already been explained, as a plain sewing stitch, on page 18. Use it as an outliner in embroidery, like drawing with a dotted line. If the design looks a bit feeble, it's surprising how a second line of stitches

MUSIC

running parallel to the first will liven it up. It is also rather effective to lace another coloured thread in and out of the stitches (just the stitches, not through the fabric). Transform a sweater that you're tired of by embroidering a simple straight-line design like this in thick wool. When embroidering knitted garments always work loosely so that your sewn stitches will stretch as much as the knitted ones.

A plain lightweight shawl looks very pretty with a flowery design worked in running stitch with fine threads.

Backstitch

(Also detailed on page 18.) Another line-maker; this time a continuous, as opposed to a dotted, line.

With many of the embroidery stitches that follow a straight line or go along an edge you will find it easy to keep the stitches even and all the same size if you chalk fine guide-lines first.

Blanket stitch

Blanket stitch has already been explained on page 21; as well as using it for an edging, you can work it into lines or shapes. Also you can vary the length of the stitches for a different effect.

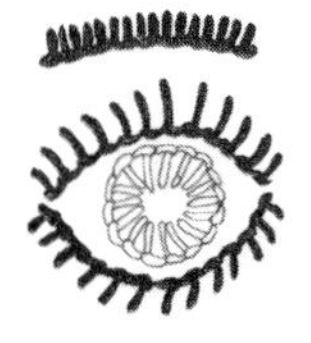

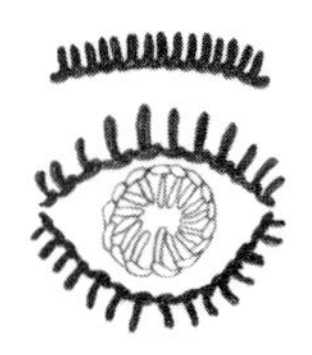

Feather stitch

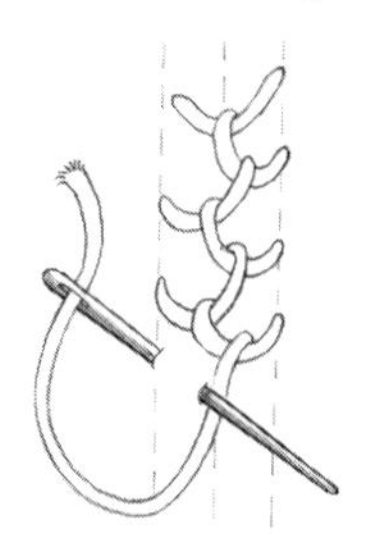

This is done like blanket stitch. Blanket stitch has little straight legs sticking out on one side. Feather stitch has little sloping legs sticking out on each side. It's helpful to chalk three lines, one each on either side and one through the middle. Work as with blanket stitch, by passing the needle through the loop each time but sew each stitch at a slant.

Chain stitch

This is good for making heavy lines – in fact, chains. To start off bring the thread through the cloth and hold a loop of thread down with your thumb. Push the needle back in again just to the right of where it first came through. Let it pick up a short length of fabric and pull it out again, over the loop. That makes the first link of the chain and you just repeat that process. Don't pull it up tightly or the fabric will pucker and your chain will look all mean and nasty. (Mind your thumb! Bloodstains are hard to wash out.)

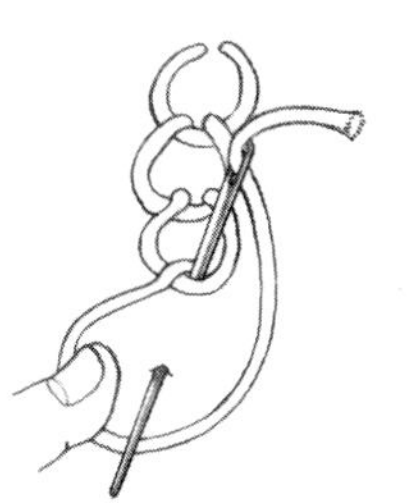

Chain stitch can also be used to fill in shapes. Work a chain round the outside of the shape first and then go round and round working inwards until you fill up all the space.

Lazy daisy stitch

Sew a loop, just as for chain stitch. Instead of going on to make another loop, do a tiny little stitch over the bottom to hold the loop down. This is traditionally used for doing flowers – daisies, would you believe?

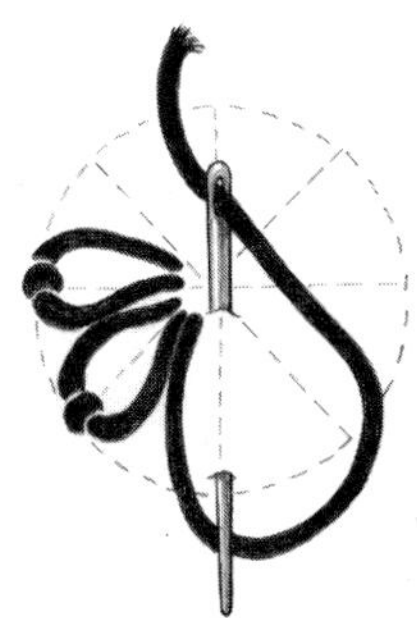

To make a daisy with the petals evenly distributed first chalk a circle (round a coin or something) and then divide it across with lines on which to centre the petals.

Use single daisy stitches in a row (or rows) as a border too.

Herringbone stitch

Herringbone can be used for single lines. By working a number of rows next to each other you can get a good-looking lattice effect. Work the row between two drawn parallel lines. Pull the needle out at the beginning of the bottom line and push it back through the fabric on the top line, to make a big diagonal stitch. Make a small stitch backwards along the top line. Pull the thread out to make another diagonal, crossing the first one. Take a small stitch backwards along the bottom line . . . and so on.

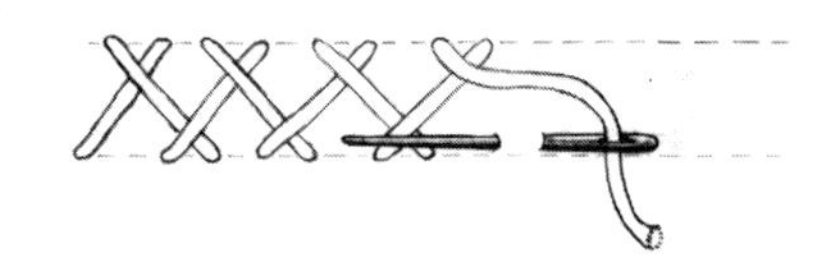

Cross stitch

Again, this may be used for lines, borders, etc., but it can also be built up to fill in an area, more solidly than herringbone will. Once more, parallel lines are a help. Sew a row of one slope of the cross first. Then come back doing the opposite slope. Keep the needle vertical.

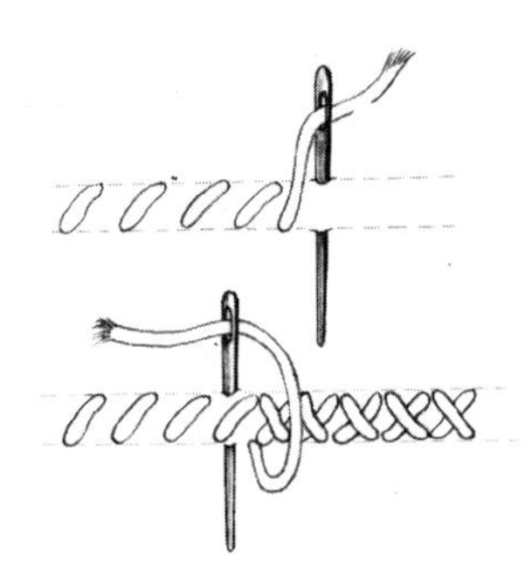

Satin stitch

This is a delicious way of filling in a shape with solid colour. You just keep sewing parallel diagonal stitches across the shape. Make them close together (gaps look awful) and keep to the edge of the design carefully. If it's more suitable to do so, work in two or more sections, rather than torturing yourself to keep it neat.

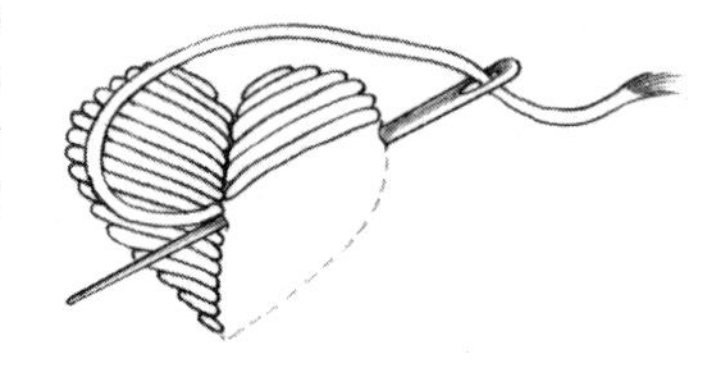

Speckling

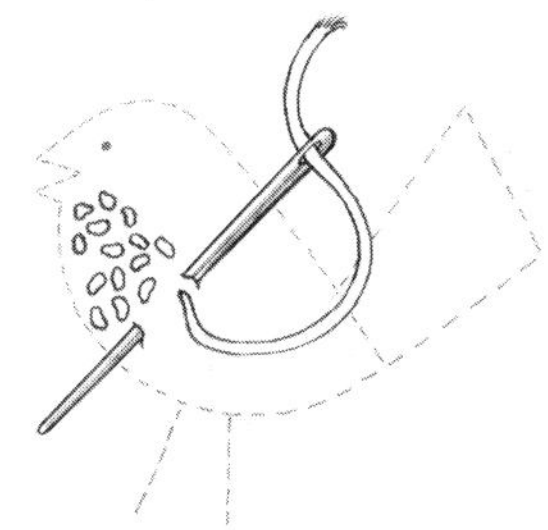

You may not want to fill an area in solidly, but to give it a texture. Try speckling. You do a tiny satin stitch and then another one on top of it. Then, leaving little gaps in between fill the area with speckles, all scattered in different directions.

French knots

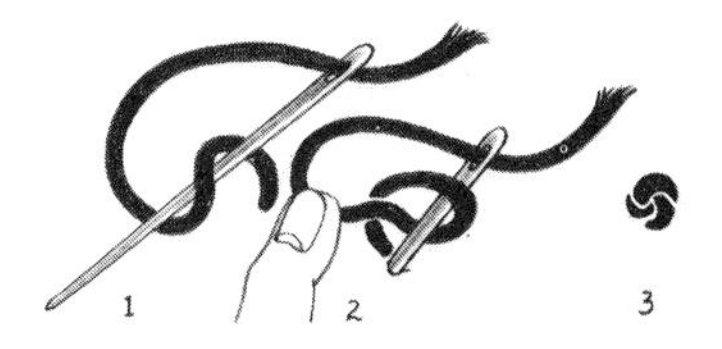

These are little bobbles. Pull the needle and thread through the fabric. Twist the thread round the needle. Hang on to the thread with your thumb and take the needle to the back where it first came out. Pull it gently into a knot (you can let go now).

Couching

Sometimes it's fun to give a design a really bold outline. Couching is how you attach, with stitches, either a number of threads forming a cord or an actual cord, length of wool, etc. Arrange the cord so that it follows the outline of the design. You don't have to do it all in one go but, if it helps, pin down the bit you are dealing with. Then, with a thinner thread, in the same or a different colour (depends what effect you want) make small, even stitches over the cord, every 1cm or so. For a more elaborate effect use little groups of over-stitches or something fancy, like cross stitch.

To lose the ends of the cord effectively thread them through to the back of the fabric (make a small hole to poke them through if necessary) and secure them with some tiny stitches.

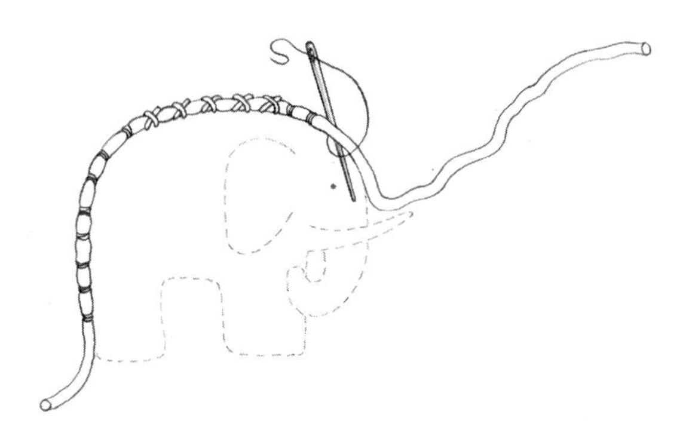

Using the sewing-machine

If you are able to use a modern machine the handbook will tell you all about the different stitches and embroidery effects you can get. But if your machining is confined to Granny's hand-operated old faithful you can still have great fun with designs done in lines of straight stitches, using your normal sewing threads. It's rather like drawing with a ballpoint pen.

Try it out first on a bit of scrap cloth – just some lines, wiggles and zigzags. When turning direction sharply (as at the bottom of a V) keep the needle down through the material, lift the foot and gently swing the fabric round so that it will be in the right position when you lower the foot and start to sew again.

This linear (that is, made of lines) type of embroidery can be employed as a delicate trimming – perhaps just a few parallel lines in a subtle colour, echoing the edges of a garment:

Or you can create an extravaganza with gorgeous different coloured lines. It combines beautifully with painted areas of fabric too.

Sew-ons and so on

There are many well-known forms of sewn-on decoration you can use effectively – sequins, braid edgings, piping with cord and trimming with lace or fringes. Here are some more unusual ideas.

Hardware

Have you heard of the pearly kings and queens? They're leaders of the London barrow boys and they wear a traditional costume covered in little pearl buttons, all arranged in patterns. You could copy this idea. They needn't be just pearl buttons – collect any and every kind of button. Then sew them on all over a jacket, for instance. Mix in pin-on buttons, brooches and badges too, if you like.

Speaking of buttons, just simply changing the buttons on a garment for some more exciting ones can work wonders. Or putting loads more on (they don't need buttonholes); and they can also go on normally button-free areas as decoration – round the edge of a collar, for example.

Different types of chain are sold in craft shops (for jewellery) in haberdashery departments (for millinery chain) and in ironmongers (for lavatories?). It's an interesting way of outlining shapes.

Metal decoration particularly suits jeans and jean jackets. Bought studs and metal eyelets are easy to apply (they press or hammer in, instructions on the packet). Needlework and toy shops sell fascinating toymaking accessories like bells and eyes and noses (even ears).

Be ingenious and sew on found (that means free) bits and pieces – old keys, curtain rings, paper clips, washers, bolts, little cog-wheels, etc.

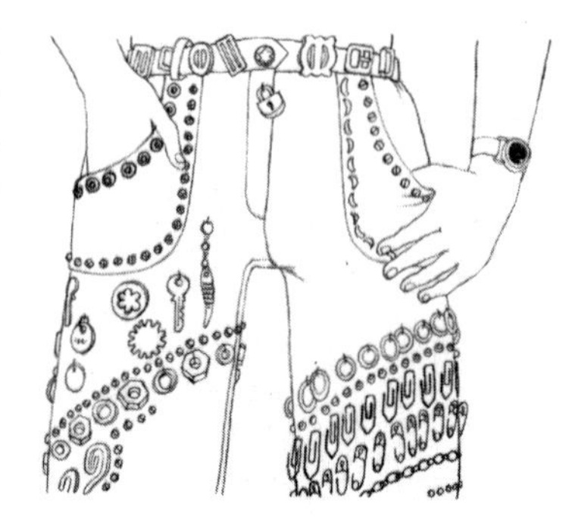

Any and every kind of bead can be sewn on – plastic, wooden, glass, pearls and sparkly rhinestones. It's an excellent use for broken necklaces. Try working beads in with embroidery stitches too – or with appliqué (page 170). Depending on the design, you can sew beads on separately or in strings. Use a fine flexible needle for tiny ones.

To sew beads on separately do a little stitch between each bead:

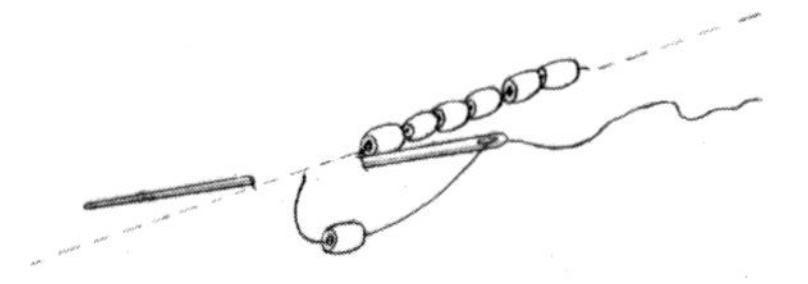

To sew them on in a string, thread a few on the needle and then take a small stitch before threading up the next lot. Don't thread too many at a time, especially if they are heavy beads, because they will hang down in loops.

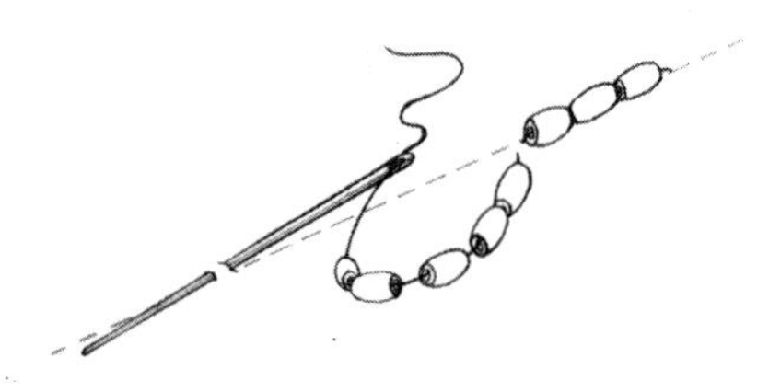

For speed, but not for guaranteed washability, use Bostik 1 to stick sequins, etc., on to clothing.

When on holiday, or if you live near the sea, comb the beach for shells and tiny stones with holes in. They are surprisingly common. Use these too for sew-on decoration.

Software

Grannies, jumbles and charity shops are all rich sources for seemingly useless bits of lace and embroidery. You'll come across little mats, doilies, long things called table-runners, curiously-shaped bits of embroidery that never reached their intended destination and, if you're lucky, maybe a lace collar or cuffs. Seize them. Generally they are incredibly cheap because nobody (but you, with your little book) can think of anything to do with them.

The little mats make stylish pockets sewn on without any alteration. Collars and cuffs can, of course, be used for what they are.

If you have pieces of lace that are badly damaged, cut them by cutting round the edge of the motifs, not straight across the fabric.

Complete cut-out lace motifs look lovely on clothing as pieces of decoration – so do cut-out embroidered motifs. Iron-on bonding material is a wonderfully easy way of applying them. Use a damp cloth that doesn't matter and can be thrown away afterwards because the adhesive will come through the holes in the lace or around the cut-out shape on to the damp cloth. However, it won't show at all on the garment. This is also a clever way of attaching braid, rick-rack, etc. Follow the instructions on the packet (and refer to page 19) and you'll have the smartest trimmings in town – and positively no sign of any glue. It's the answer if your sewing is inclined to be a trifle wobbly.

Think how you can incorporate an odd piece of embroidery into a garment, sewing it on or ironing it on.

You might concentrate on lace-collecting and make yourself a complete dress or a top and skirt from accumulated lace pieces. (Don't forget tablecloths, tray-cloths and bedspreads.) If you manage to make your garment entirely from hand-made lace you could end up with a museum piece worth a lot of money!

Lace can be bleached and also dyed. You can also do interesting things like threading ribbons in and out of it or adding tiny beads.

Fabric and plastic flowers and feathers (real or plastic – for the latter, see the photos on pages 37 and 41) are valuable materials, decoration-wise. If the fabric flowers are all squashed, having been at the bottom of the hat stall, revive them by holding them in the steam from a boiling kettle.

Have fun decorating things with woolly pompons (page 29) or mad little woolly people like you made when you were tiny.

Posh patches

You fell off a bike and your knees suddenly said hello through your jeans. You thought you were deftly negotiating the barbed wire until a nasty ripping sound rent the air – and the back of your jacket! You simply wore through the elbows of your sweater by constantly leaning on the desk. All cases that call for patching – but not just boring old matching patches. Make the patch itself a little work of art so that it no longer simply looks like something covering up a hole. In fact the patches look so good that you'll find you want to use them as decorations in themselves, not merely as repairs.

Make sure your patches are in fabrics that require the same method of washing as the garments you are patching. Don't, for example, apply a 'dry-clean only' fabric patch to jeans which are likely to be frequently in and out of the washing machine. Also, patch in a fabric of a similar weight to the garment.

The basic idea is to cut out a shape of the patching material that's bigger than the hole. If your machine will do a zigzag stitch things are really simple. Pin or tack the patch over the hole and sew it on by zig-zagging round the edge with very close together stitches. The zigzag stitch then becomes what is known as satin stitch. You don't need to turn a hem under because the closeness of the stitches prevents the fabric from fraying. A similar result can be achieved by hand if you use button-hole or blanket stitch – stitches again very close together. Sew with wool or embroidery thread – whichever goes best with the garment.

With this method you can cut the patch to any shape you like. This is called 'appliqué' which means 'applied' in French, and there are lots of different ways of doing appliqué. One effective idea is to cut out carefully round a motif (that is a complete picture of something in a design such as a bird or a flower or a bunch of flowers) from a printed cloth and appliqué it with a closely stitched edge.

Try painting, printing or embroidering your own patches too. All these techniques are explained in detail in this book – just look them up in the index at the back. Do your design on the patch before stitching it to the garment.

Stick-on patches

You can stick patches on. If you are patching over a big hole it's advisable to cut out a piece of thin material just slightly larger than the hole. This goes on the inside of the hole as a backing patch; the fancy patch goes on the outside, with the part of the garment bordering the hole sandwiched in between. The reason for this is to stop the glue going through the hole. Imagine a hole in the knee of your jeans. Without the backing patch you could stick the front and back of the trouser leg together for ever.

One method is to use a fabric adhesive which is sold in hardware and do-it-yourself stores. This can be rather messy, so do as they tell you on the instructions otherwise you will stain the fabric. Lay the patch in position on the garment and lightly draw round it. Put a VERY sparing coat of adhesive all over the drawn shape. Don't slosh it on. Be mean with it. Coat the back of the patch in the same sparing way and, if you are using one, the edges of the backing patch too. Let the glue dry. When all the bits are dry assemble them carefully in their correct positions. They will stick immediately so you can't mess about. Put a piece of scrap paper on top and press the patch down firmly. This adhesive will wash all right but don't dry-clean it – it disappears and all your patches fall off.

The other way is to use a bonding material which is a web of sticky stuff on a special sheet of paper. You can buy it in a haberdashery shop. In pencil draw the shape of your patch on the paper. Cut roughly round it. Following the instructions on the bonding material packet, place the cut-out piece, paper side up, on the wrong side of the patch fabric. Iron it to melt the adhesive and make it stick on to the fabric. Let it cool off and then cut the shape out round the pencil outline. Peel the paper off. Put the patch, right side up, in the right position on the garment. Lay a damp cloth over it and iron it. This melts the adhesive again and bonds the patch to the garment. This adhesive is both washable and dry-cleanable.

You can simply stick your patches on by either of these methods, especially if the fabric is not inclined to fray. For a more fancy look add decorative embroidery over the edge of the patch – and more around the outside if you wish. You can really go to town on these edgings, making them most elaborate. Work in all sorts of combinations of blanket stitch, chain stitch, feather stitch, couching and herringbone (page 160).

Felt, suede, leather and suedette

Patching with materials that don't fray at all means, of course, that you don't have to worry about trapping the edges under close-together stitches. Felt is fine for patching woollen sweaters and cardigans as long as when the time comes for you to wash them you do it carefully, by hand, in lukewarm water and mild soap. Before making a felt patch it's a good idea to check that the colour doesn't run in water. If you are patching a place that will get a lot of wear it would be better to use some other material, especially if your felt is rather thin.

Leather and suede make superb patches. You could cut up an ancient garment – one that's beyond repair – or use the leather from a worn-out handbag. A chamois (shammy) leather duster makes ideal patching material. For where to find felt, suede and leather see page 14.

Thickish leather or suede patches can be stuck on with fabric adhesive (as explained above) but you can sew on the thinner type. Pins or tacking stitches will leave permanent holes so pin or tack only round the edges where any holes will later be covered by stitching. To make sewing easier on either leather or suede use the machine without any cotton in the needle to run a line of little holes round the edge of the patch. You can then hand sew it on in and out of the holes however you like.

Any of these methods can be used to bind cuffs or the edges of cardigans and sweaters that are a bit the worse for wear.

Get into print

Ever thought of printing on your clothes? It's the obvious way to put a message over.

Use printing too for an absolutely limitless range of patterns. Here are some ways of doing it.

Printing blocks

The word 'block' is applied to anything that will print. You put colour on it; press it on to the material and it leaves an impression. It's exactly the same process as when they rubber-stamp things in the Post Office. Perhaps you've done lino-cutting – just the same. You can make your own block but you can also use existing things. Just have a look around. The end of an ordinary round pencil (providing it isn't chewed) will give you this shape:

The other kind of pencil, this shape:

So already you have two motifs that can combine into a border or edging. One of the great things about printing is that you can easily repeat the printed image. So by doing it over and over again you can quickly build up a design.

Once you start looking you'll find loads of odds and ends that are ready-made printing blocks.

What do you print with?

Obviously the print must be washable. There are special dyes, paints and printing inks on sale in art shops. Fabric paint, such as Dylon Color-fun, or fabric dye paste, like Rowney's Fabric Dye, work well on many objects, particularly anything with water in it like half a pear. This is because paint or dye will mix with water but fabric printing ink won't. Acrylic paints can be used but if you apply them too thickly they'll make the fabric rather stiff.

Fabric printing inks, which are oil-based, make the cloth a little stiffer than fabric paints or dyes do. But they pick up fine details beautifully (see the feather), and you can use them very successfully for printing on paper too (Christmas cards and such-like).

How to print

Wash and press the fabric or garment first – this applies both to old things that may be dirty and, most particularly, to new things because new fabric contains dressing that will prevent the colour penetrating the fabric properly.

Have some scrap cloth to practise on first. Don't throw these try-outs away – see why later.

To print on material you need the following set-up (minus Pussy).

Lay a piece of old blanket or a soft layer of newspapers on the table but watch out you don't print over any creases. The purpose of this is to give a slightly yielding surface for the block to press into. Spread out your beautifully ironed piece of material or clothing. If it's the latter, slide some paper inside under the area to be printed in case the colour goes through. You don't want to print the other side by mistake. Have some more newspaper handy.

Using paints or dyes

Either apply the paint or dye to the block with a brush or use a stamping pad. This is simply a thin piece of plastic sponge. Splodge some colour on to it. Press the object being printed on to the pad so that it becomes coated with colour. To print an object like a pencil end carefully press it down on the fabric; lift it away – and it will have left its impression. With a leaf, or something similar, first lay the leaf, colour side down, on the material. Put a piece of newspaper over it and gently but firmly press down all over the leaf, through the newspaper, to be sure you've transferred the complete image. Remove the newspaper and peel away the leaf.

When you've finished printing clean up the brushes, etc. with water.

If, by accident, you get a blob where it shouldn't be QUICKLY *remove it by washing that spot first in cold water and then in hot water and detergent. (Or you could deliberately turn it into a ladybird or a flying saucer or something.)*

The prints should be allowed to dry thoroughly. For dye-prints you iron them to fix the dye to make it washable. Details on the jar tell you how to do this.

Fabric printing ink

You'll need some rags and some white spirit (turps substitute) to go with this – the spirit is both to dilute it slightly if it's very stiff and for cleaning up afterwards. You can brush it on but the most enjoyable way of using fabric printing ink is with a roller (which can be bought in an art shop).

You'll need an inking slab – a small piece of formica, glass or hardboard. Squeeze a line of ink on to this and, rolling in different directions, spread it out evenly with the roller. To print a flattish object, place it on a bit of newspaper and roll the ink from the inking slab on to the object. Keep doing this until it's thoroughly inky. Print as described above. To ink a solid object hold it in your hand.

Accidental marks can be removed if you act speedily with plenty of white spirit and a CLEAN rag.

When your printing session is over clean everything up properly with white spirit (including your hands; the really filthy should use Swarfega).

Fabric printing inks do not require any fixing procedure.

Designing and making your own blocks

In your nursery school days you probably sploshed around with potato printing. Don't dismiss it as only kid's stuff. A potato, not to mention a carrot or a turnip, makes an excellent printing block, printed with paint or dye.

Wash and dry the potato and cut it in half. With a kitchen or craft knife cut away the parts of the design that you don't want to print, leaving the printing bits in relief. If you have any lino-cutters you may like to use them instead of a knife.

With this kind of printing everything comes out as a mirror image, so if you want to do letters, they must be backwards on the block. In fact, doing words and initials is more straightforward using stencils (explained on the next page).

A rubber eraser is a good base for a relief printing block. You have six flat surfaces to use. Cut away the unwanted parts of the design with a craft knife.

Linocuts are very successful printed on clothing. Use fabric printing ink applied with a roller. The old-fashioned thick kind of lino is best. Keep a look out for people who are taking it up and putting down new floor coverings. You can buy pieces of lino in art shops but this is clearly more expensive. Try chatting up an art teacher. The cutters, which are little gouges, are also available in art shops – if you can't borrow any.

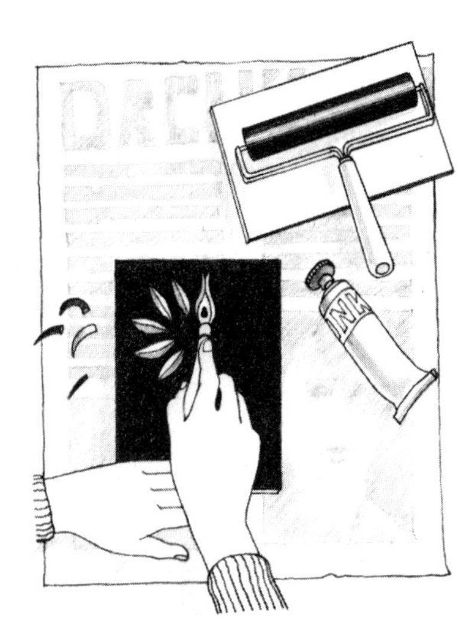

One word of warning: when gouging lino keep the hand holding the lino BEHIND *the cutting hand, then, should the tool accidentally slip, you won't cut yourself.*

A different way to make a block with the design in relief is to start with a piece of stiff card and to stick things on to it. Use a strong, all-purpose glue, like Bostik 1, and stick on cut-out felt or card shapes, string, bits of lace, sacking, buttons, hair-grips, matchsticks, in fact, anything you like.

Stencilling

For doing words it may be worth buying a set of stencil letters (they're not very dear) but for designs and patterns it's fun to make your own.

You'll need some thin card (cornflakes packets are ideal), a pencil, a sharp craft knife and something to cut on – a sheet of glass or thick card.

Work out your design and then, before you cut it out, check to see if there are any places where little tags may be needed to hold the pieces of the design together. For instance, you couldn't stencil this flower without tags to join the centre (an unprinted part) to the outside edge of the flower. When you cut out the design the centre would fall out and you'd get:

So leave little card tags like this:

Having checked all that, carefully cut each section out with your knife. (Incidentally, a sharp craft knife is much less dangerous than a blunt one. It's the blunt ones that slip.)

Once again have the same table layout as for block printing. Use fabric printing dye or fabric paint (not ink) for stencilling and apply it by dabbing with a small piece of sponge. Try a dummy run on your test cloth. By applying less and less pressure with the colour-soaked sponge you can achieve some good shading effects.

If it helps, lightly tailor's-chalk where the design is to be. This is particularly applicable with lettering. One danger to watch out for is, by mistake, sponging colour over the outside edge of the stencil or through an unwanted section (particularly on bought lettering stencils). To avoid this, first place the stencil with the appropriate bit in the right position. Then put pieces of newspaper over any potential danger zones, while you stencil the part you require.

Spraying through stencils gives fabulous results. You dip an old toothbrush in the dye and, holding it bristles up, scrape a knife across the bristles towards you. This shoots a spray of colour on to the stencil.

Practise first. Don't go and immediately ruin your new sweatshirt with horrible uncontrolled blobs. Remember to fix the designs for washability.

Combining techniques

Mixing methods together gives you great possibilities. Think of spraying a vague, misty background of mountains and clouds; introduce some trees done by printing leaves; add some block printed people and embroider their faces – sequins for eyes and little pearls for teeth . . . stop, stop!

Transferring

This is like magic. It's also very easy. Magazines and newspapers are printed with ink that is very similar to fabric printing ink, which, if you recall, is diluted with white spirit – that's its solvent. If you soak a magazine photograph in white spirit you loosen the ink. You can then, by rubbing, transfer it from the magazine page on to your T-shirt or whatever. You can't get as strong an image as there was originally in the magazine, but you could make a beautifully romantic, slightly unearthly collage of your favourite group, or wear your own personal print of your current hero. Here's the technique.

Because the image is light use a white or very pale coloured garment. Test it first by using another photograph torn out of the same magazine and applying it to somewhere inside the garment where it doesn't matter.

Drawing-pin the garment out flat on a hard surface – NOT the best dining-room table, though! Soak the photograph, on both sides, with white spirit – slop it on with a brush or a paper tissue. Leave it for two or three minutes, lying on some newspaper.

Place the photograph, face down, on the material and fasten it with two drawing-pins at the top. With something smooth, like the handle of a knife, rub firmly on the back of the picture. Lift it to see if it's working – the pins ensure that it will flop back again into the right position. If it's working, carry on systematically rubbing until you have transferred all you want to. You can slosh on more white spirit if it seems to be drying out too much.

If it isn't working, don't tear your hair. This means white spirit is not the solvent for that particular ink.

Newspapers and the cheaper types of magazines work best with white spirit. For stubborn photographs experiment with different solvents – try lighter fuel or methylated spirits.

When clothes with these prints need washing do it gently by hand with mild soap and avoid rubbing the printed area.

Fabric crayons

You can buy these in a craft shop. Read the packet first because some brands suit only certain types of fabric. You draw your design on paper with the crayons – making sure it will fit the space intended for it on the garment. Pin the drawing face down on to the material and iron the back of the paper. This transfers your design on to the fabric. These crayon prints are washable.

Using up your test pieces

All your odds and ends of test prints make an interesting patchwork. (Don't forget to fix any that require it.) Mix them in with plain or patterned fabrics.

Another idea is to use a single printed motif as a decorative patch on its own. Patchworking techniques, page 120; posh patches, page 170.

Painting

You can paint directly on to fabric. 'How to transfer a design on to fabric', page 141, explains how to transfer a temporary outline on to your material. Use fabric paint or paste-consistency dyes for a soft feel. (Don't forget about fixing them afterwards.) Acrylic paints make the fabric stiffer but they are fine on an already stiff fabric like heavy denim.

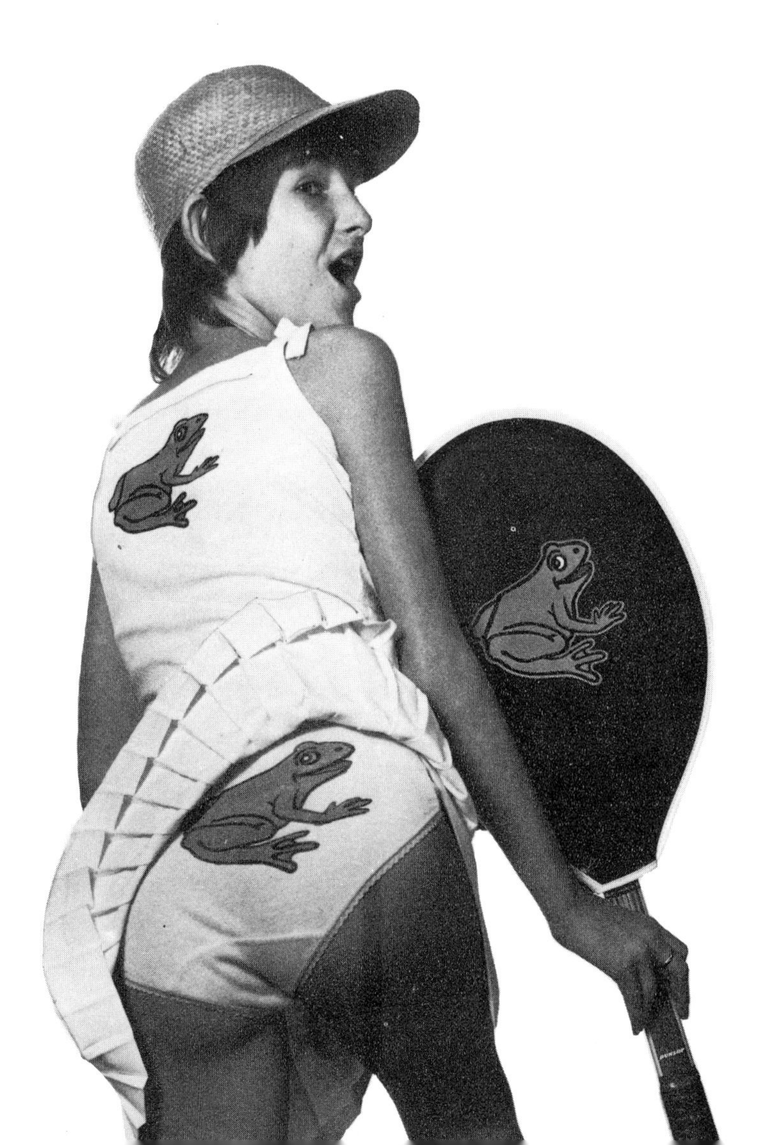

Paint literally any subject you like – whole scenes, patterns, animals or visual jokes like this:

As with printing, slide some paper inside the clothing so that the paint doesn't go through and spoil other parts. Keep the material pinned out taut; it's much easier to paint on then.

If you've fixed the paint according to the manufacturer's instructions then it's quite safe to wash the clothes in a washing-machine.

Useful points

Addresses

Dryad Ltd produce an excellent and truly vast range of every kind of craft material plus handy books and leaflets. Their extremely comprehensive catalogue cost £1.50 in 1979. (What about splitting the cost of the catalogue and subsequent mail orders with friends?) Write to or visit Dryad Ltd, PO Box 38, Northgates, Leicester LE1 9BU. Dryad merchandise is also available direct at Binns of Hull, Humberside, and Reeves Dryad, 178 Kensington High Street, London W8.

Dylon Ltd make a wide range of dyes for home use. Any problems – contact their Consumer Advice Bureau, Dylon International Ltd, Sydenham, London SE26 5HD.

Hobby Horse Ltd, 15–17 Langton Street, London SW10, stock super craft goodies which you can mail order. Send a stamped, self-addressed envelope for their fascinating catalogue sheet.

The Victoria and Albert Museum, South Kensington, London SW7, is full of things to give you creative ideas. The museum also publishes books and booklets on subjects such as embroidery. These are obtainable at the museum or through booksellers or any of Her Majesty's Stationery Offices. Have a look round any museums, etc., in your local area too.

Woolworths supply all manner of useful things such as fabric adhesive, iron-on bonding materials and cheap tape.

About the garments shown in the photographs

You may like to have some more information on garments in the photographs. Page 41 shows a shirred top and skirt in batik patterned material and a very quick-to-make party dress with stuck-on sequins, etc. The dress on page 119 has patchwork bands around the upper sleeves to match the lengthening patchwork. The quilted tabard on page 133 and the dress on page 153 are both tritik designs by Jane Callender. On page 159 many of the basic embroidery stitches are combined to produce a rich design. The cardigan on page 163 is enlivened by a swarm of bees embroidered in satin stitch and backstitch. On page 167 the beaded jacket is a rare jumble treasure; the sailor's smock is decorated with table mats; Jacky and Nicky discuss how to use their jumble finds; lace oddments trim a plain navy sweater. On page 173 the large areas of the design on the patch pocket are stencilled, the small patterns are printed with blocks cut from a carrot. The baby's hat on page 177 is potato-block printed. Page 183 shows how you can copy a motif on to your clothes in fabric paint.

Metric/imperial conversion

All the measurements in this book are metric; if you prefer to work in feet and inches it is useful to remember the following approximate conversions.

1 inch – 2·5cm
1 foot – 30cm
1 yard – 91cm

Index